GW01454456

Poetry in Motion

Kent

Edited by Steve Twelvetree

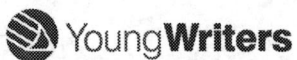

Young**Writers**

First published in Great Britain in 2004 by:
Young Writers
Remus House
Coltsfoot Drive
Peterborough
PE2 9JX
Telephone: 01733 890066
Website: www.youngwriters.co.uk

SB ISBN 1 84460 344 X

Foreword

This year, the Young Writers' 'Poetry In Motion' competition proudly presents a showcase of the best poetic talent selected from over 40,000 up-and-coming writers nationwide.

Young Writers was established in 1991 to promote the reading and writing of poetry within schools and to the youth of today. Our books nurture and inspire confidence in the ability of young writers and provide a snapshot of poems written in schools and at home by budding poets of the future.

The thought effort, imagination and hard work put into each poem impressed us all and the task of selecting poems was a difficult but nevertheless enjoyable experience.

We hope you are as pleased as we are with the final selection and that you and your family continue to be entertained with *Poetry In Motion Kent* for many years to come.

Contents

Aylesford School

Cator Park School For Girls

Rebecca Ashton (11)	50
Shannon Ellis (11)	51
Molly Cox (11)	51
Alice Jones (11)	52
Caitlin Johnstone (13)	52
Kim-Chi Bui (12)	53
Cordelia Scott (11)	54
Melanie Nagle (13)	54
Lisa Wennell (12)	55
Hannah Partington (11)	55
Larissa Barnett (11)	56
Nisa Cooper (13)	57
Sinead Castineira (12)	58
Zoe Williams (12)	58
Poppy Feakins (12)	59
Johanna Francois-Walcott (12)	60
Bianca Denise Forde (12)	61
Sarah Cullen (14)	61
Alda Krasniqi (12)	62
Tammika West (12)	63
Kylie Graham (15)	63
Acacia Northe (12)	64
Anna-Louise Johnson (11)	64
Abisola Akinbowale (14)	65
Kelisha Vincent (12)	65
Monique Tulloch (12)	66
Kloé Dean (14)	67
Chelaine Young (15)	68
Victoria Studd (14)	69
Nabisa Sulaiman (14)	70
Katie Eastop (14)	71
Marsha Gayle (15)	72
Kaylie Rule (14)	73
Grace Pepper (14)	73
Rachel Fryer (14)	74
Robyn Burge (11)	74
Yolanda Shaw (14)	75
Lynsey Steedman (14)	75

Chatham Grammar School For Girls
Jayde Balderston (11)	76

Jennifer Shannon (13)   76
Stephanie Shaw (12)   77
Rebecca Reay (12)   77
Angela Davey (13)   78
Emily Henderson (12)   79
Emma Richards (13)   80

Christchurch CE High School
Laura Davies (13)   81
Jay Sage (14)   81
Billy Charles (13)   82
Hayley Simmons (13)   83
Aiesha Carter (13)   83
Damion Maskell (13)   84
Luke Stonham (13)   84
Danielle Taylor (14)   85
Danny Bradshaw (13)   86
Lee Pearce (13)   87
Barry Blackall (13)   88
Maxine Goldsmith (13)   88
Stephen Staras (13)   89

Cobham Hall
Tomi Fadoju (12)   89
Angeliki Kosti (14)   90

Dover Grammar School For Boys
Oliver Carpenter (14)   90
Connor Lehan-Finn (12)   91
Jack Gregory (12)   92
Liam Petch (12)   93
Jeremy Delsignore (12)   93
Zak Fisher (15)   94
Jared Wills (12)   94
Benjamin James Curtis (12)   95
Sam Elliott (12)   95
Sam Cooke (12)   96
Alex Williams (12)   96
Ryan Doble (12)   97
Robert Stewkesbury (12)   97

Jake Sandford (12)	98
Thomas Etheridge (12)	99
Nicholas Odell (12)	99
Moamen Nasr (12)	100
Lewis Hook (12)	101
Michael Bushe (12)	102
Nicholas Saunders (13)	102
Daniel Allen (13)	103
Leslie Hayden (12)	104

Dover Grammar School For Girls

Hannah Wales (14)	104
Sinead Chapman (12)	105
Emily Turner (13)	105
Abigail Hall & Jenny Lovell (12)	106
Samantha Sheppard (11)	107
Jennifer Ashcroft (12)	107
Charlotte Hyde (12)	108
Sophie Biot (12)	109
Anne Plumridge (13)	110
Rachel Gisby (13)	111
Ryanne Robertson (11)	111
Catherine Watts (11)	112
Georgia Beverton (12)	112
Robin Dyer (12)	113
Racheal Haddon (12)	114
Loren Selby (11)	115
Georgia Broadhurst (11)	116
Amber Tonkin (12)	117
Louisa Love (12)	118
Katy Spice (12)	119
Fay Goddard (12)	120
Sian Smith (11)	121
Jessica Capon (12)	122
Lisa Mannings (14)	123
Iona Joy McCarvill (12)	124

Hartsdown Technology College

James Liam Taylor (11)	124
Mary Elizabeth Bull (11)	125
Emma Palmer (11)	126

Abbie Jayne Morrison (11) — 126
Mark Blake (11) — 127
Sophie Scargill (12) — 127
Imogen Culliford-Morcom (11) — 128
Samantha Evans (11) — 128
Nadia Kerrigan (13) — 129
Chanelle Smethers (12) — 129
George Flegg (13) — 130
Chris Tazey (12) — 130
Tom Solly (13) — 131
Nathan Smith (12) — 131
Abbie Bridson (12) — 132
Terry Peake (11) — 132
Gareth Mason (11) — 132
Levi Baker (13) — 133
Lauren Miller (12) — 133
Eleanor Katherine Thain (11) — 134
Megan Sara Brackenborough (11) — 134
Benjamin Whisson (13) — 135
Kier Buchanan-Cox (11) — 135
Toni Paul (11) — 136
Robert Adrian Watts — 136
Mark Baker (13) — 137
Ricky Lee Lambert (11) — 137
Rachael Barker (13) — 138
Abby Aldous (13) — 138
Ben Akhurst (13) — 139
Rochene Turney (13) — 139
Rhiannon Ayles (13) — 140
Alice Freeman (13) — 140
Portia Godden (13) — 141
Natalie Orr (13) — 142
Emilie Arnold (13) — 143
Carina Banham (14) — 144
Ysabelle Bradshaw (13) — 144
Ella Chapman (13) — 145

Helen Allison School

Aaron Barnes (14) — 145
Marc Fosker (13) — 145
Richard Langworthy (16) — 146

Conor Rourke (12)	188
Stuart Smitherman (12)	189
Danial Morgan (11)	189
Grant Eldridge (12)	190
Katrina Reynolds (16)	190
Chris Martin (11)	191
Robert Campbell (12)	191
James Smith (11)	192
Sarah Back (13)	192
Michael Dance (12)	193
Daniel Horton (12)	193
Nicole Gardner (12)	194
Myles Tichband (12)	194

Rainham School For Girls

Chelsea Penn (12)	195

St Anselm's RC School, Canterbury

Thomas Childs (11)	195
Thomas Dewey (12)	196
Isla Cross (12)	197
Sarah Tutt (11)	197
Rebecca Stiffell (11)	198
Stephanie Gawler (11)	198
Peter Matthews (11)	199
Hugh Molloy (12)	200
Zoë Buckland (11)	200
Anna-Lisa Stiffell (11)	201
Kate O'Leary (11)	201
Natasha Usherwood (11)	202
Thomas Solley (11)	202
Lucy Vallely (11)	203
Jessica Belfiore (11)	204
Sophie Mitchell (11)	205
Solumtoochi Ebenebe (11)	206
Alice Crocker (12)	207

Sir Joseph Williamson's Mathematical School

Daniel Ostridge (11)	207
Balwinder Singh Rangi (11)	208

The Poems

The Gary Ward Rap

You have turned the page and fallen into my trap
Now you're gonna have to listen to the Gary Ward rap.

I was born on the 7th month of May,
Oh I remember that awful day!
I was tucked up in my mother all nice and tight,
You couldn't see nothing because it was dark as night!
It was so warm, I didn't want to leave.
Then something pushed me at 20Gs!
Ten minutes later the doctor gave a shout,
'One more push Mrs Ward and he'll be out.'
I said, 'This doesn't look like a stalk?'
The doctor said, 'Lord, he can talk!'
I popped out my head, 'Now watch me walk.'
I waddled and shuffled around the room.
I slipped and landed on my head with a boom!
The doctor put me on her lap
She took out the medicine and gave me a night cap.
So I went to sleep and that's that!
That's all I can remember, and you've listened to . . .
The one, the only,
Gary Ward rap.

Gary Ward (13)
Aylesford School

The Blackout

As black as the phantom's cloak swishing in the night,
As black as the raven flying in the cold midnight air,
A huge cloud of blackness and despair fills the skies,
Black mist engulfs the outer core of the world,
Shrouding and encircling the earth,
A dark lord sucks the light from the tiny planet,
Forming a big dark hole in space.
He maliciously grins at the swirling black ball
Hanging in the atmosphere . . .

Andrew Small (10)
Aylesford School

The Daughter Of Hell

People call me 'Satan's Pride', 'The daughter of Hell' they said,
But did they know the freckly, rosy, laughing child
who skipped upon the green?
Did they know the beloved daughter who played with the
merry village children, their laughter ringing like bells
while her mother baked them cakes?
But here I am. I am blamed.
A poor, filthy peasant, cold and quiet, sweet memories hidden
and sheltered, covered by pale and wounds. Wounds they gave me.
Why is all taken away when all I had done was help?
I wandered, carrying only herbs in my pockets, keeping to myself.
They made stories up, said I was evil from the start. I stood by the
Devil and watched him spread a pointed, red hand over the earth.
I aided him, I brew bloody wars and sang songs of suffering
mercilessly. Heartlessly.
They say I poured carcass skin and pickled roaches in
cough medicine and gave it to the children. They say I stole
Honey-coloured stars in wells, clothes and babies' toys.
I was penniless. Never to be wealthy. Though poor, I was proud.
I loved. I was loved myself, but they will not think that when they
see the woman hanging in the square, rope around her neck.
Old and worn. Left to rot.

All they will say is, 'Witch' . . .

Nicola Clark (13)
Aylesford School

Horrors Of The World

Everywhere and nowhere,
nowhere and everywhere,
death cannot be seen or heard,
and yet you know it's there,
whether it's being hit by a car,
or through a disease.

Hallowe'en is the time of darkness,
where dark spirits walk the Earth,
when it's not Hallowe'en, the spirits are crushed,
beneath the Earth, called Hell,
but on Hallowe'en they walk
amongst the living whether you
see them or not.

Boil, boil, boil,
if you have led a good life
you go to paradise,
but lead a bad life, you go
to a living nightmare.
One of these will come to everyone
so be careful which path you choose.
Death stalks you at every corner.

Ian Sagar (11)
Aylesford School

3-2 I Think I Saw A Scouser Cry

The game was Charlton verses Liverpool
The score, it was 3-2
The defence, it was a shambles
They didn't have a clue

Lisbie, what a game he had
His finest ever hat-trick
To win this unexpected game
To make the Scousers sick

Houllier was very angry
His team wasn't very good
He tried to blame everyone else
But then we knew he would

As Charlton climb the table
Into 11th place
I think they will out-do Liverpool
In this year's title race.

Luke Flight (14)
Aylesford School

September

Usually a cold and damp month
but this year is different
as the sun is shining
the berries are ripe
and the conkers are falling
the mushrooms are ready
to be picked
leaves on the trees are still green
the flowers are blooming
as the bees are collecting nectar
it's the month of a new school year
the days get darker
this is a good month for fishing
also for golf.

Jordan Hayes (11)
Aylesford School

School

Teachers
Nasty and mean
Should be heard
But not seen

Lessons
Boring and archaic
Should be colour-washed
Like a big mosaic

Homework
Mindless and time consuming
Unhappy and clueless

Detention
Monthly after school
I try to avoid it
But I am a fool!

Gavin Barton (15)
Aylesford School

On An Autumn Day

Autumn is the time of year,
Leaves are dropping, autumn's here,
Golden coloured leaves,
Falling from the trees,
On an autumn day,
Twisting, twirling,
Floating, falling,
The leaves drop this way,
On an autumn day,
Leaves falling from the trees,
Blankets of leaves for all to see,
Conkers drop from the trees,
So kids can play and be pleased,
On an autumn day.

Kayleigh Sparrow (14)
Aylesford School

The Place I Want To Be!

The place I want to be,
Is somewhere near the sea,
Where a sunny day,
Brightens you up in every way.

The place I want to be
Is nowhere near the sea,
And where fluffy white clouds
Fill the deep blue sea-looking sky.

The place I want to be,
Is a place where I feel free,
And where there is no one to bring you down,
And treat you like a clown.

But to be honest,
I am already where I want to be,
Near my family and my six true friends,
I mean the place you really want to be,

Is truly in your golden heart!

Lauren Keen (13)
Aylesford School

Autumn

As I battled my way through the leaves,
Rustling and crunching,
Leaves fluttering gracefully to the ground,
Spiders' webs glistening in the morning sun.
As squirrels and hedgehogs prepare for winter,
The smell of bonfires consume the woods.
Conkers, acorns and hazelnuts scattered along the leafy ground.
Leaves brightening up the dull, bare, gloomy woods.
People picking elderberries.
Coming up to the big moment.
Harvest festival!
Days become shorter.
Mornings become colder.

Charlotte Blackaby (11)
Aylesford School

The Burning Candle

I light a candle for you.
When I was alone you were there.
When I had no one to talk to you were there.
When kids were teasing me you were there.
Wherever I went you were there for me.

My candle is burning.
You would walk with me barefoot, if I don't have shoes.
You would talk to me when no one would.
You didn't care what I looked like.
You would make me warm if I was cold.

The candle died.
I'm looking for you in the playground.
I'm looking for you in class.
I'm looking for you in town.
I'm looking for you everywhere.

Where have you gone?

Suzaan Datema (14)
Aylesford School

Friends

Friends are like scars, they stay with you forever,
They surround you with love and affection and never let you down,
But until one day that scar disappears,
It's hard to find another just like that,
So you have to take a break, sit down and think,
What was it that I did that changed the thing we had?
I remember the times we had together,
At school and then after, and now they're lost.
Now I know we took our own directions,
New lives, new friends, we had a new start.
The years have passed, but I'll find a new friend,
One that's kind and caring,
But the friend I find will never be you.

Reanne Hammell (13)
Aylesford School

Friends

Friends are always there for you,
They help you in whatever you do,
We talk to each other all the time,
Don't blame me if this doesn't rhyme!
We may moan,
We may groan,
But we're never off the phone!
We sit and chat,
We may have a spat,
But in the end,
We'll always be friends!
We meet in town,
We shop and shop 'til the sun goes down,
We party all night,
From dark to light,
And sleep through Sunday mornings!

Katie Stannard (13)
Aylesford School

Life Vs Death

Life continues to root and tangle itself through our world,
Our planet, Earth, as through space it is hurled,
Yet as fast as it grows, life is slowing,
As if a force is to stem its flowing.

People would deny that life is fleeting,
For it is human life that is not caring,
Factories, guns and people are going,
It is this we are knowing.

Many will soon see that we are beheld by death,
The world is in its autumn, there will be no more breath,
War, plagues are what we bring, are the doing,
Gone are many lives, we know we are destroying.

Phil Sagar (14)
Aylesford School

My Love Poem

I thought you were smart,
but then you broke my heart.

I thought you were the one,
but now we're done.

You cheated on me,
but I didn't see.

We went to the movie,
we thought it was groovy.

We had that picture taken,
what I see when I awaken.

You made me cry,
when we said goodbye.

I didn't believe myself to start,
then I saw we should never be apart.

I had to keep going over us,
but I didn't want to make a fuss.

You were my lover,
but became my cover.

I was devoted to you,
I didn't know what to do.

I couldn't believe you'd left me,
because we were meant to be.

Now I'm in English writing this poem,
I met someone new, but I hardly know him.

Laura Jayne Sales (15)
Aylesford School

A Day In The Life Of A Cat

I am a cat named Berty
I roll in the mud and get dirty
I have smooth, soft, silky fur
And when you stroke me I let out a loud purr

I'm told I have a cheeky grin
Especially after my owners catch me raiding the bin
Once I've eaten all of the leftover curry
My owners laugh and watch me trot to the toilet in a hurry

At day I hide in the grass waiting to pounce
Then as I catch my prey I give a gleeful bounce
I waddle with my present all the way home
I drop it at my owners' feet and lay down expecting a comb

At night I shut my droopy eyes and curl into a ball
I know I look so cute and so small
I get a cuddle and a kiss goodnight
My owner leaves, looks back and turns off the light.

Rebecca Amos (15)
Aylesford School

Life

Life is long and hard,
At most times everyone hates it.
You get up most mornings not wanting to live it,
But when you think about it, you love it,
You love the way people treat you,
You like the way you live at home,
You laugh and cry all through life,
But yet you say you hate it,
Avoiding all bad things is not a real life,
Good always comes after bad,
That's the way life goes,
Life is like a road, not knowing what's to come,
Bumps, turnings, accidents and crashes,
Until it just stops.

Kay Sharp (13)
Aylesford School

War In Iraq

Disaster has struck
As the war starts
People crying
With broken hearts.

Children want their daddies back
Wondering why
There's a war in Iraq.

Smoke and clouds
Cover the sky
Bombs go *boom!*
Women cry.

Children want their daddies back
Wondering why
There's a war in Iraq.

Everyone's praying
It's going to be alright
Hoping Iraq
Will give up the fight.

Children want their daddies back
Wondering why
There's a war in Iraq.

People are dead
People are alive
Some died
Some survived.

Stephanie Curtis (12)
Aylesford School

The Frustration

I don't know why the curse gets worse as the time goes by
I have more tribulations than a mental patient
No one sees the struggle, they only notice the trouble
They don't see the depression, they only see the bad impression
That's why I do bad things as an expression
It seems that no one can see my violent dreams
No one can hear my silent screams
No one can feel my pain
Even on a sunny day I feel rain
I wish the creator would just erase me from this cruel place
He'll never embrace me
My adversaries will always face me
I wish I could stop my bad ways and wish for better days
Not a well done, not even a praise
I hope this is just a phase.

Tahssin Mahammad (15)
Aylesford School

The Year

Birds of nature flying south
a little animal filling his mouth
golden tears becoming bare
animals at night getting a scare

Snow of winter filling the land
a hibernating animal clutching his hand
flowing river turning hard
two inches of snow filling the yard

Over the freezing land the snow is silent
starving animals becoming violent
the animals think the end is near
the snow and clouds begin to clear

The animals and trees begin to bloom
so many babies but there is plenty of room.

Michael Timson (13)
Aylesford School

Goodbye

A week ago you were ill
The nurses made you take a pill
Seeing you lying there made us cry
But in the end we said goodbye

Although your time with us is gone
The memories we have will still go on
Mum said you would be watching over us
She said you will always be with us

In the end you said you weren't the best
But as grandparents go you were better than the rest
Now you're up there with Nan
Tell her I miss her, if you can

Time is short, you have to go
But before you leave, you have to know
That I will always think of you
And the others will do too.

Rachel Baker (14)
Aylesford School

Autumn

Autumn is the time of year,
that really gets you going,
crunchy leaves and rich brown conkers,
bright red colours, scarlet and brown.

Autumn is the time of year,
harvest festival I like to hear,
crunchy hazelnuts and blackberries too,
leaves are fluttering down by you.

Autumn is the time of year,
bonfire smoke and cold, frosty air,
glistening spiderwebs in the trees,
oh what a beautiful scene to see.

Nicole McDonough (11)
Aylesford School

Things That Go Bump In The Night

The shadowed figure that cannot be seen
Moving swiftly through the streets unclean.
Breaking the silence with blood-curdling screams
Coming to take a small boy's dream.

Alone at night
Shrouded in fright
Cos the bumps you hear
Are getting near.

They're almost at your bedroom door
Boards are creaking in the floor
Are these frightening noises real
The mystery that you can feel.

The handle's turning
The candle's burning
The beast comes to take the light
I'm paralysed, I just can't fight.

Are they the beasts under your bed
In your closet
In your head?

Nick Cradduck (14)
Aylesford School

Honeybee

Your honey sparkles
Like a gold ring,
Your sting is shiny
Like a very, sharp pin.
Your black stripes glisten
Like a pitch-black night,
Your body is curved
Like a lovely, round circle.
That's all I can say about now -
For now and forever, ta, ta and ciao!

Sema Asim (11)
Aylesford School

Hallowe'en!

The worst time of the year is Hallowe'en,
It always makes me shiver and dream.
Not pleasant dreams but scary things,
Like witches' hats and Devil's wings.

Not forgetting ghosts and ghoulies,
Spiders and the creepy-crawlies.
The long white fingers and nails too,
Vampires' blood all to scare you.

The cold wind blowing in the dark sky,
The shining bright moon way up high.
Pumpkins flaming on window sills,
Anything more to give you the chills.

The bangs and knocks upon your door,
Looking through the spy hole, just to be sure:
There's nothing that scary to make me shout,
Or the bats in the air that fly about.

As I lay here tucked up in my bed,
Horrid thoughts are running through my head.
As you can see, on Hallowe'en,
It always makes me shiver and dream!

Lauren Cayless (13)
Aylesford School

Winter

When the wind blows
The sunshine goes.
Flowers rot
In my pot.
The fire is burning
And kids are yearning.
Everything turns white
As if by fright.
This is the beginning of a winter's night.
I wait and wait
And anticipate
Hoping that Santa comes in his sleigh
Which I will raid.
Once he was there
I was snuggled up to my bear
And was asleep
Thinking of sheep.

Maria Anderson (13)
Aylesford School

Autumn

Autumn is the season of colours
Everybody's getting prepared for the winter that's going to come.
Dark red
Scarlet
Gold
Crunching leaves, frosted grass
The crops are being collected
The stock is being protected
The harvest festival's coming soon
Pure white is the moon
Spiders' webs glisten in the sun
Autumn, it's the time of fun.

Christopher Hatch (11)
Aylesford School

Running Race

On your marks, get set, go.
The crowd all sat in a row.
The gunshot went.
What an exciting event.
Will just broke his toe.

There's now seven in the race.
Will's got mud over his face.
Oh dear, we've lost.
We're all very cross.
All because of his stupid pace.

He's now off the track.
We're thinking of giving him the sack.
The race is now near the end.
Will lost on the first bend.
We all knew he had started to lack.

On your marks, get set, go.
The crowd disappeared from their row.
The gunshot had been fired.
Will had retired.
And it's all because of his toe.

Jack Turner (13)
Aylesford School

The Hounds Of Winter

In the dark they bring fright
And creep beneath my veins tonight

They hide the howling shrieks within
Let the scars start to thin

They bare teeth fierce in their head
To tear the flesh and make blood red

The beauty maiden we shall not see
For dead among the thorns she'll be

In the forest black as black
Calm the seas, let that be that

For the moon can do no wrong
It is where our hearts belong

As a star, it lights the sky
Don't let the one you love pass by.

Maria Goodhew (13)
Aylesford School

Mary

Eyes of the wolf,
My grandfather says,
She is different from the rest,
She is calm, unspoilt by hardship,
I watch her, she is mystical,
Captivating,
I make no sound as she gracefully undressed,
She slipped into the pool in one fluid motion,
Her body is perfect and untouched
By hardships of life,
She is a picture of perfection,
Her scent is one of wild flowers and
Dew in the morning.

Andy Hall (13)
Aylesford School

School Street

As I wander through the school,
I hear people talking in the hall.
People running like they are in a race,
Too much of a blur to see their face.
Everyone outside a classroom they wait,
Not wanted a detention so they can't be late.

I would prefer to talk to my friends all day,
And listen to what they have to say.
Stopping off at a classroom, I open the door,
When I'm in, I wonder what it has in store.
It is the last lesson, but has felt like a year,
Thankfully the end of the subject is near.

Some of the information comes off me,
If I was a bird then I would be free,
I pack up my things and wait for the bell,
Because I can't stand another second in this tight fitting cell.
Restless people start to roam,
I hear a ring, it means time to go home.

Charlotte Stowell (13)
Aylesford School

Autumn

The leaves start to turn brown
As they fall off the trees
The animals collect their stock for the winter
The nights are longer
As the days get shorter
The farmers collect in their harvest
As we all trick or treat
Conkers start to fall off trees
Bonfire night's coming real soon
The weather starts to get colder
That is autumn.

Scott Oliver (11)
Aylesford School

Oh War, Oh War, It Is No More

War is bloody,
War is hell,
War is where my good friends fell.

As I watched the bullets fly
People fell and people died.
Once I reached the muddy beach,
I knew my life was at its breach.

We made our move,
For the enemies' line,
And hoped we wouldn't run out of time.

The bullets flew,
The cannons roared,
We moved and crawled upon the floor.

We lay upon the muddy beach,
Until the death of people peaked.
It was then I realised the idea of war,
That claims the lives of many more.

The waves now calm and the guns asleep,
The lives of many friends have reached,
Their first and final eternal sleep.

Now I know the truth of war,
The evil lurks for evermore,
The thought of evil,
And the thought of war,
Will not trouble me no more, no more.

Robert J Hutton (14)
Aylesford School

Important Days Of December

December is here,
Christmas is near,
the presents have already appeared.
3 days away,
it's time to display,
the fairy and the Christmas tree.
The Christmas tree's glistening,
while Mum and Dad are listening,
to the sound of Christmas carols.
Christmas has now gone,
New Year is not long,
for another great celebration.
New Year's Eve is here,
no presents to receive,
12 has struck for another great year.

Jade Angelique Summers (11)
Aylesford School

Autumn

Red, orange, deep red and brown,
These are the colours I see,
Walking through the woods.
In the early morning, there's frost around,
Glistening webs, glistening leaves,
Brown hard conkers lying on the ground.
I kick them out of my way,
And walk on and on,
Then I see more conkers and acorns.
I watch the different coloured trees,
I watch the open fields,
Then I see a couple of busy bees.
I head back and see all the things I saw,
All the different colours,
I wish I could see more!

Jack Cheeseman (11)
Aylesford School

Spring

Early this morning I awoke,
Lying cold and quite still,
Thousands of birds flew past my windowsill,
They sang so loud but understanding,
And the words they spoke of were so demanding,
They spoke of people, laughter, all so undone,
And to me it brought up the morning sun.
Seeing new animals makes me feel content,
Just beginning to walk on the freshly smelling cut grass,
Sweet, tender, peaceful and scented.
Their mothers and fathers seem so proud,
As the animals jump around,
Then they disappear into the immense crowd.
All the trees, plants and things all begin to grow,
New crops are growing, waiting for the coming harvest,
Even though my country life seems so low,
I know in time everything will be normal once again.

Natalie Newman (11)
Aylesford School

Things That Happen In Autumn

Autumn is different coloured leaves, falling off trees,
Yellow leaves, brown leaves, orange leaves an
Many more.
Autumn is raking the leaves off the grass like a
Dog chewing on meat with its sharp teeth.
Autumn is having picnics in the garden
Under the tree.
Autumn is when the leaves gently fall to the ground
Like a feather floating to the floor.
Autumn is children playing chase in the park,
Like squirrels running about,
Autumn is my kind of season.

Kerry Baber (11)
Aylesford School

My Best Friend

My best friend, Sophie,
She's tall, cool and clever,
She makes me smile
When I'm under the weather.

There's no one like Sophie,
She brightens my day,
Her smile's in my heart
Throughout every day.

My best friend, Sophie,
With her long blonde hair,
She has always looked after me,
And really does care.

There's no one like Sophie,
She's there through tough times,
That's why I'm so glad
That she is just mine.

My best friend, Sophie,
She loves all her family,
But sometimes I wish,
She was just here with me.

There's no one like Sophie,
After all we have been through,
That's why I promise, I promise
I will never forget you.

Laura Gilbert (12)
Aylesford School

The Soldier

(For a British soldier who yearns to be back home with his family)

Dawn
and the soldier is woken
to the sound of the TV
in his head
and the odd car passing his house

his children playing
and getting ready for their first day at school
the sun rising slowly
from the east
of his small precious town
but always comes back

reluctantly, reluctantly

comes back to roadworks
of a frightening blood-red war
to massive explosions
to early mornings and the feet are sore

dreaming, dreaming
he dreams of his family
the soldier prepares to fight

another day at war.

Matthew Newbury (14)
Aylesford School

My Future World Of Hopes And Dreams

I look into the future, life not as it seems,
Impossible to live my life based on hopes and dreams.

Floating houses, dreams on Mars,
People who hate chocolate bars,
Tall people, short people, fat and thin people,
People with hair down to their knees,
Eyes like stars, feet like trees!

School on Jupiter, shops on Mars,
Then there's houses in the stars,
The sun leaves my world with no night or day,
So all the people cannot lay,
So all day, all night their eyes stay bright.

They look at the world in which they live,
Looking at the life in which they breathe,
My world that's based on hopes and dreams.

Isla Stigle (12)
Aylesford School

Autumn

Autumn, autumn, it's finally autumn
when the leaves fall off the trees.
They cover the ground with red, orange and brown,
the colourful leaves of autumn.

Wild animals hibernate and migrate through the autumn's coldness;
squirrels searching, gathering their nuts to prepare
for autumn's coldness.
Summer flowers disappear
days are getting shorter.
Hallowe'en is nearby
fireworks are closer.

The leaves no longer sit upon the trees so tall
they look so bare standing there,
swaying in the fresh autumn air.

Francesca Hammon (11)
Aylesford School

A Poem About Witchcraft

The sound of the chanting,
The screams of the terrified,
The bubbling of a cauldron,
The light,
The bang of the potion,

Many run in fear,
In fear of being killed,
Many scream,
Many shout,
They shout, 'Kill her,
Kill her, she's a witch.'

You'll have to prove it,
You'll have to prick me,
Find my numb spot,
Float me until I sink,
That is if I do,
I don't mind.

Confess I won't.

Danielle Redgrave (13)
Aylesford School

Autumn

Autumn is when colourful leaves brighten the floor,
Autumn is the battle of the trees and the wind,
Autumn is when evergreen survives to add to the beauty of nature,
Autumn is when multicoloured leaves cling to your feet,
Autumn is the last hope of warmth, as the purifying cold
creeps in towards winter.

Alan Clarke (12)
Aylesford School

Autumn

Autumn is the time of year
when leaves fall off the trees.
Autumn is the time of year
when leaves start to freeze.

Autumn is the time of year
when Hallowe'en is the night.
Autumn is the time of year
it sure gives people a fright.

Autumn is the time of year
when Guy Fawkes has returned.
Autumn is the time of year
when bonfires are going to burn.

Autumn is the time of year
when squirrels gather their nuts.
Autumn is the time of year
when conkers come out of their huts.

Autumn is the time of year
when nights are always longer.
Autumn is the time of year
when the days are always shorter.

Ryan Laker (12)
Aylesford School

Heavenly Christmas

(This poem is dedicated to anyone who has lost a loved one)

Christmas time's upon us,
And there's one thing that is clear,
You won't be here to decorate the tree with us this year,
But as we think of you at this time and push away our fear,
Of spending Christmas without you,
Like this one, year after year.
Thinking of the memories that we had, back then,
And wishing that the times we had could come around again,
We'd hang garlands around the mantelpiece,
And decorate the tree,
Every year at school the nativity scene
Was done for all to see.
We went carol singing in the cold,
And we sang them to the young and old,
There were lights around the window, their fires glowing bright,
And where were we? Outside singing,
On a cold and frosty night.
Our presents wrapped so brightly and hidden cautiously,
Dad hid them in the cupboard so us kids couldn't see,
What did we have for Christmas? We'd wonder every year,
There would be presents Christmas morning,
Of that there was no fear.
As we lay in bed this Christmas eve and find it hard to sleep,
We'll be praying that your Christmas in Heaven
Is like the memories we keep,
So this Christmas we'll remember just how it used to be,
Year after year we will cry a little,
We won't forget you see.

Rebecca Best (15)
Aylesford School

Roger's War

My name is Roger Rat Fate
Of regiment 28.
I fight the war with hope and glory,
But it just keeps getting gory.
For example, take the time
While I was waiting in line.
A bullet flew,
Hit the loo,
And bounced into my wine.
That was the end of the booze,
Or the war we'd surely lose.
So I took up smoking,
But started choking,
And court-marshalled I shall not choose.
So in conclusion,
In confusion,
War is not that nice.
The English are building Spitfires.
The Germans are building tanks.
The Americans are building fridges.
And the French are losing ranks.
Hitler's mum is bombing London,
Hitler's dad is dead.
What the rest are really like,
That is what I dread.

Thomas Mockford (12)
Aylesford School

The Hanging

The rope tied,
But the tears I hide.
I see the crowd,
Their cries are loud.

As the hood is lifted down,
The last thing I see is her frown.
She looks so scared but prepared.

They cut the rope,
I hear her scream.
My legs start to shake because all I know is that I'm a fake.
I have no one, I'm alone in the world.
I stand here all alone, shrivelled and curled.

I miss her already,
What shall I do?
This hanging was deadly.
This whole thing was all very cruel.

Where shall I go?
What shall I say?
These are all questions,
Is this how it will stay?

I turn to the darkness,
I can no longer see her face.
She has gone forever,
We will never be together ever again.

Lauren White (13)
Aylesford School

December

December is a special time
crackling fires
flashing lights
having lots of snowball fights

December is a special time
Christmas trees
singing songs
partying all night long

December is a special time
opening gifts
a Christmas wish
special food on every dish

December is a special time
frozen hands
chilly faces
visiting many special places

So December is a special time
and here I said it all in rhyme.

Amy Mason (11)
Aylesford School

The Ring Of Life

They believe in circles
The ring of life
There's no start
There's no end
Just the ring of life

They believe in circles
Just like the wedding ring
There's no start
There's no end
The ring of life within.

They believe in circles
Just like the shiny sun
There's no start
There's no end
When the ring of life begun.

Sophie-Leanne Jeffery (13)
Aylesford School

Sailing

Set sail across the sea,
Across the Atlantic or perhaps the Pacific.
Enjoy every breath you take,
Looking back to the past, you must never do.
Everyone has ups and downs,
Like the waves on windy days.
Spread your wings and fly away,
Don't get lost with the calm currents,
Everyone can get drifted away,
By the gentle waves.
For a couple of days,
The sea is your home.
You must never feel alone,
As there are fishes under your feet,
And birds flying above your head.

Chayara Begum (13)
Aylesford School

The Journey

The journey is long,
the path is unknown.
We will follow the friends,
and follow the foes.

The waves rock the boat,
sending you to sleep.
The babies are crying,
and the mothers weep.

For me there is no one,
to hold my hand.
Or waiting for me,
at the promised land.

The journey is at its end,
the night has come.
Is someone there for me?
Anyone?

Hannah Burnett (13)
Aylesford School

Witchcraft

Everyone sleeps soundly but I lie wide awake,
There's someone else in here, I feel my legs begin to shake.
I can hear her footsteps creaking on the stairs,
I can hear her empty breath from a witch who isn't here.

I keep quiet lying on my bed,
If I try to scream, I'll surely be dead.
I can see her cat, as black as night,
Its yellow eyes make me wish I could take flight.

She's on my landing now, creeping to my room.
I look out of the window and I can see her broom.
She is in my room and she pushed the light switch,
She is my mother and she is an all powerful witch.

Harriet McCann (14)
Aylesford School

Native American People

We people, live here,
We hunt with spears.

One day a strange ship arrived
And we had to change our lives
And so we were deprived.

Days went by when we were hungry and thirsty,
Whites took our food away today.
We trade and argue and kill.
Over here, every man for himself
But our warriors use stealth.

Our people will suffer and fight the enemy
Oh Lord God help us!
The whites are making such a fuss.

Today we were kicked off our land,
Right till the end of the sands.
We are sad,
We have done nothing bad!

Luke Shacklock (13)
Aylesford School

School

School's important so I'm always told
people who tell me they're all old

Every morning I start the day tidy
you should see me by the end of Friday

All the teachers go really mad
that's because my class are so bad

Get done for always chewing gum
in return I have to do a long sum

Trying my luck with the girls by flirting
then the teacher comes along and say, 'Tuck you shirt in.'

After lunch I line up for assembly
it's so crowded it's like being at Wembley.

Whoops! I forget to do my homework on pensions
Oh no, it's the dreaded 'after school' detention!

School's at last over, the bell rings
'Yippee!' everybody cheers and sings.

Robert Knight (12)
Aylesford School

Man Of The Road

Midday
And man of the road sits up
To the look of fortune in his eyes
The steady but sure
The calm but slow
The poor becoming rich

From bricks to cardboard
From marble to stone
All round and plump
To a bag full of bones

Fresh carvery
And slaves and maids
The sun's rays bouncing off his eyes
From streets to the countryside
From this world of fortune
He always comes back, slowly but surely

Comes back to gold and shimmering heights
A grey dull path
The echoing of traffic and footprints besides his head
With brains like his, he sees where he should be

Coughing and sneezing
His crumpled bag rustles
Future seems clear
From streets to countryside in less than a year

Another dreary day.

Amelia Blackman (14)
Aylesford School

Ruby

Everyone has a moment
A time in this darkness to shine
Everyone needs a reason
To prevent themselves running blind
But I feel her suffering
And I lose the will to live
For her to just be happy
What more do I have to give?
Memories are like butterflies
They evolve and fly
How do I continue
When I just want to surrender and die?
The rungs of my ladder are worn
The pedestal shook
But when I gaze into her face
She gives me that same, old look
To stand and be noticed
Or to fall and fade away
And I regret the time I ran and hid
Stroking the skin with the blade
Will of a loved one is not something to dismiss
For dreams do come true
Though not through a wish
To beat or be beaten
To sink or to swim
She will conquer and never fall
The brightness of the light of the unjust
Is now finally fading dim.

Laura Louise Batt (16)
Aylesford School

Devastation Strikes

The plane comes crashing
People dashing
Some too late
9/11 the date

Families broken
Innocent lives stolen
New York changed
Hearts just drained

People jumping
People crying
Fire blazing
City sky hazing

Children missing Daddy
Young ones in a paddy
News teams dashing round
People running, homeward bound

Just be grateful you're still here
And pay your respects
just once each year.

Sarah Howland (12)
Aylesford School

Monty

I'd like to share a tale with you
About a friend I love through and through
He takes my side in every fight,
And sits by my bed, night after night

He looks at me with big, brown eyes
And when I leave he sits and cries
He hates it when I'm out at school
He'd rather I was home, playing ball

He doesn't like the cold, prefers the heat
Really hates rain, snow and sleet
He likes it when it's warm and sunny
Sunbathes all day (and looks quite funny)

So how did I meet this loyal mate?
Was it at school or on a date?
No, it was an animal rescue home
Where someone had left Monty all alone

To you he's just a shih-tzu cross
To me he's a friend and also the boss.

Grace Barrett (12)
Aylesford School

The Race

This is my day, this is my race
Today is the day I'll win first place

As I approach the line my nerves come out
The race is all I can think about
The man on the side, raises his gun
Today is the day I'll be number one

This is my day, this is my race
Today is the day I'll win first place

And then it happened, I heard that bang
I lifted my head and instantly ran
It was ever so thrilling
At last I was winning

This is my day, this is my race
Today is the day I'll win first place

I could hear the crowd crying
I felt like I was flying
I could hear my rivals very near
It felt like this race was taking all year

This is my day, this is my race
Today is the day I'll win first place

I was chasing the finish
At last I could win this
When I reached the end
The world was my new best friend

This was my day, this was my race
Today was the day I won first place!

Sam Morrison (15)
Aylesford School

Lonely Boy

(For a lonely boy whose friends only live in his dreams)

Night
a lonely boy falls asleep
of the sound of joy and laughter

hundreds of his friends
playing together all day
the thrill of running around
passing a ball
in his exciting land
but he always wakes up

to cries of other people's laughter
and hurtful prodding and poking from bullies
spinning round him like a spider's web

shaking
he drags himself out of bed
and stands on his skinny bruised legs
slowly, slowly
he drags himself through

To another judgement day.

Samantha Burrows (14)
Aylesford School

What Do I See?

I see a person who looks very white,
I see her in the middle of the night.
I see her with a bright, white gown
And I see her without a frown.
Her eyes twinkle like the stars
She looks like someone from afar,
Her hair is bright blonde like the sand
On a Caribbean island.
She reminds me of a lovely, white dove
Then I knew she was an angel, from above.

Danielle Randall (12)
Cator Park School For Girls

Recipe For A Haunted House

First put in a mug of darkness,
Then add a little death wish.
Next sprinkle in a few cobwebs
Then deliver a killer bed.

Don't forget to add some ghouls,
Then put in some moving walls,
Next throw in a pinch of scare,
Then dash in a ghost, without a care.

Add in a few vampires,
Then add some electric wires.
Next dash in a couple of bats,
Then mix in some evil cats.

Put in a green, warty witch,
Then darkness, black-pitch.
Throw in some bones,
Plus a skeleton that moans.

Add in some kills,
Then put the house on a hill.
Finally add a rotten, dead mouse,
Then you have . . .
A haunted house!

Lily Kim Sing (11)
Cator Park School For Girls

The Sea

The waves crash against the shore,
Tide drifting in more and more.
Water rushing at my feet, faster and faster,
Just washed off my new toe plaster.
As night falls, I rush to the pier,
The sea is near . . . the sea is here . . .

Elizabeth Alaka (11)
Cator Park School For Girls

Recipe For Friendship

1	Gallon of love
5	tbsp of trust
3	tsp of sugar (for sweetness)
5	handfuls of understanding
3	puffs of hope for the future
7	cups full of loyalty
3	squeezes of lemon (for fun)
13	pounds of funny jokes for sleepovers
10	hugs for encouragement
15	kilos of good gossip
5	alibis to get your friend out of trouble
£50	to spend on chats on your mobile
3	spoons full of charity
8	good magazines to read together
70	tbsp of spice (to spice up your lives).

Jessica Fitch-Bunce (11)
Cator Park School For Girls

A Star

So
Shiny
So bright
I love to glow and   light up the night!
I'm awake when people sleep. It's like
the day is yours and the night is
mine to keep. What am I?
A star! A star so far in
the dead of night If it wasn't for
me you   wouldn't see
as I'm   just like
a   light

Harriet Rogers (11)
Cator Park School For Girls

I Think Cats Are Cute And Cuddly

Their whiskers are long, like straws,
Their ears are as pointed as a triangle,
Their claws are as sharp as pins.

I thin cats are cute and cuddly.

Their chins are bony like rocks,
Their noses are as sweet as tiny buttons,
Their fur is silky, like silk.

I think cats are cute and cuddly.

Their eyes gleam like stars at night,
Their faces are small and round, like an apple,
Their pads are as soft as beds.

I think cats are cute and cuddly.

They jump like mice with no sound,
Their paws are as dainty as ballerinas.
Their tongues are rough, like sandpaper.

I think cats are adorable!

Sophie Barr (11)
Cator Park School For Girls

Angels

They wear a robe that is silky white,
They are a blinding sight.
When I met him, I couldn't move,
The way he gazed I think he knew
As he hovered above me.
There were his wings that I could see,
He said, 'I have to give you this ring.'
I wondered why he was giving me this certain thing.
I went to ask but he had already gone
And there this light shone,
And there I saw an angel.

Shenelle Bardall (11)
Cator Park School For Girls

Then She Was Gone!

As the wind howled its frosty breath
and the trees stood frozen,
a girl walked through he darkness
on a very cold, Christmas night.

She shivered and quaked
and wrestled the trees through the forest
as though she were on puppet strings.

Then as she wandered across the land
in the pitch blackness of the night,
she flew above the windy sky
and landed in a wood.

As the frost stared in wonder
and the trees stood witness
they turned round the corner
and then she was gone!

Rukaya Ellison (11)
Cator Park School For Girls

Angel

As she strolls, cloud to cloud,
the flowers start to sing,
every step she takes, the sun starts
beaming, getting hotter by the second.
The stars twinkle when she stirs in her sleep,
her halo is golden when her eyes awaken,
the dead leaves falling from the trees,
step in mid-air to greet her.
Even on her bad days, her wings are still
as smooth as silk.
The doves cry until they meet her
on her midday walk.
The moon sits and waits, she's ready for her bed,
then he sings her a lullaby to get her into her
midnight dreams.

Shelby Murray (11)
Cator Park School For Girls

Christmas List

A horse with a tail so shiny
That's what I want!
A cute baby doll who is pretty and tiny
That's what I want!
A big, fluffy, teddy bear
That's what I want!
My own rabbit that will take a lot of care
That's what I want!
A small Christmas frock!
That's what I want!
A top up of all the Christmas stock
That's what I want!

I could go on for ever, I do want more,
But Mummy said, 'Santa, will be poor!'

Charlotte Speer (12)
Cator Park School For Girls

Nature

When I walk out into the lush, green grass,
The blazing sun's ray hits my body.
A powerful feeling sweeps over me, like a tidal wave
And my vision suddenly becomes cloudy.

I watch the trees sway to and fro
And then lie down on the dewy grass,
I stare up into the heavens above,
And think of the people who had long ago passed.

My thoughts and gratitude go to God himself,
For the things he has done for us,
And if he didn't create the beautiful surroundings,
There would be no *nature* around us.

Niyushka Ram (11)
Cator Park School For Girls

My Mum Tracey

My mum Tracey, is very bubbly,
Never drunk, always cuddly.
Shouts at me for telling lies,
But I just look at her, tears in my eyes.
She throws her arms around me, holds me tight,
Wish we could stay here, alone all night.
But she has my other siblings to love and care for too,
Besides my mum has a lot of work to do.
Washing, cleaning and brushing the floor,
Ironing, organising and a whole lot more.
To end her day, a long soak in the bath.
When she takes off her clothes, I try hard not to laugh!
I'm looking at her now . . .
But now I see her for whom she is . . .
She's my wonderful
            irreplaceable
            beautiful Mum!

Zõe Louise O'Mahoney-James (12)
Cator Park School For Girls

I Want!

I want a big bag of clothes for all to see,
A huge wad of money, just for me!
Some make-up, jewellery and a new DVD,
Or presents from friends at my birthday tea!

Or maybe a disco in a big, fancy hall,
Or shopping at The Mall!
Splashing about at the local pool,
Whatever it is, it'll be cool!

Rosie Anne Jeffery (11)
Cator Park School For Girls

My Dog Lassie

My dog Lassie is so small
Her eyes are as big and round as a ball,
Her fur is beautiful, light brown,
Her small, white feet, could walk the whole town.
She has a wet, black nose,
She has a lovely pose.

My dog Lassie is so brave,
She really knows how to behave.
She's never even broken anything,
Her ears prick up when I sing.
She has always been a star,
She know who I am, even from afar.

My dog Lassie sleeps under the watching moon,
She jumps right up when she hears a spoon.
Her tail wags from left to right,
With other dogs, she doesn't fight.
She runs up and down, really fast,
I don't remember her being so sweet in the past.

Elizabeth Morera (12)
Cator Park School For Girls

Out Of The Window

I'm looking out of the window -
What do I see?
A woman across the road, looking at me.
Something crawling over a key,
Someone paying their parking fee!
A talking parrot saying, 'Marie, Marie!'
I'm waiting now but they can't see me
Or I forgot, I'm invisible you see!

Temeka James (11)
Cator Park School For Girls

The Flame

The flame burns brightly
Flickering quickly, through the night
The flame is always shining
Burning, quietly through the night.

The orange colour, impressing eyes,
The flame lets of a strange, sweet scent.
The flame roars higher and higher
Using wisely the time that's spent.

But the wind blows harder,
The flame tries to survive.
The flame growing smaller,
It uses strength and tries to thrive.

It struggles impatiently
The flame turns blue,
It wears out
The flame is through.

Rhian Dighton (11)
Cator Park School For Girls

Water Dream

Flowing gently, calm,
Water trickles down the stream
Quiet as a fish.

Frosty, cold it's still
Transfixed on the water's gleam
Glisten in the sun.

Clear blue silk
The water is like a dress
You would wear to a ball.

Is this the water's dream?

Olivia Holland (11)
Cator Park School For Girls

Me Being The One

It involves the soft gleam
of morning light when it snows,
The sunny cool of the water
in the summertime heat.
As well as me -
being the one to watch it.

It involves the feel of water
dripping from the roof onto your head.
The freezing frost of winter
as you walk through it.
Also myself -
being the one to touch it.

It involves the sweet scent of flowers
in the morning breeze of the future.
The unmistakable taunting of a fry-up
in the morning on a winter's weekend
And me -
being the one to smell it.

It involves the sound of chirping birds
as the sun rises at dawn.
The certain chime of a school bell
as the day ends, but the locker rush starts.
And myself -
being the one to do it all.

Rebecca Ashton (11)
Cator Park School For Girls

Recipe For A Fairy

Get a bowl of water
add a pinch of fairy dust
heat it, mix it and stir it if you must.
Shake it, sieve it and whisk it in a cloud
add a sprinkle of sweet dreams
and make sure they're not loud.
Add a pinch of magic,
then freeze it for half an hour
add a bit of sunshine
and some flower power.
Defrost until runny
then add a blob of fun
then you have it right there -
a lovely fairy with
long, blonde hair.

Shannon Ellis (11)
Cator Park School For Girls

Santa Will Get It!

Pink ponies, fluffy and cute,
Santa will get it! Santa will get it!
Glittery castle, grand and tall,
Santa will get it! Santa will get it!
Blonde Barbie with shirts and skirts,
Santa will get it! Santa will get it!

Dressing up clothes, all girlie and glamorous,
Santa will get it! Santa will get it!
Big cars, fast and flash,
Santa will get it! Santa will get it!
Magic fairy wand, filled with charms,
Santa will get it! Santa will get it!
Only six months to go, must get to the post,
Will Santa get it? Will Santa get it?

Molly Cox (11)
Cator Park School For Girls

Slinky

As black as death,
As pale as night,
As silent as the waves
No one but the moon can see her,
No one sees moonlight, Slinky.
Never seen, never heard,
People wonder if she's even real.
In the element of the witches,
No one but the moon can see her,
On the rooftops with the sky,
Eyes like sapphires
She flies like an eagle,
No one sees her but the moon.
Patient as the sitting wonder,
No one sees her but the moon,
No one
No one
But the moon!

Alice Jones (11)
Cator Park School For Girls

Will You Still Be There?

If I died tomorrow,
Would you still be there?
If I got an E in maths,
Would you listen and care?
If I lost everything I had
My mum, my sister, my cat and Dad.
Would you hold your hand right out!
Would you hold me as I scream and shout?
When I'm 18, young and free
Would you walk right up to me?
So when I'm 80 and losing my hair.
Will you still be there?

Caitlin Johnstone (13)
Cator Park School For Girls

Black World

Have you ever felt that way -
Cold and lonely,
Can't wait for the end of the day,
To crawl into your warm duvet?

Away from the yelling,
Away from the fright,
To escape away
Into the blackness of the night.

Your anger is raging,
Burning inside.
Waiting, just craving
For a friend to play with.

The world is black,
Nobody likes you.
What if I ran away -
What would they do?

The world is black,
Pushed in the corner,
Nobody notices, they wouldn't care
I'm just some mourner.

Desperate for someone,
To love, I wish.
What have I done
To deserve all this?

I'm crying and screaming inside,
I'm not worth it to see
Don't hate me. Don't disgrace me,
You wouldn't know - you're not me!

Kim-Chi Bui (12)
Cator Park School For Girls

My Big Moment

It was packed and I was scared
The lights went out, it had started.
I was on!
I was on!
I was on!
It kept echoing through my head.
As I went out, I saw a sea of heads
Just staring . . . staring at me.
My mum was there and so was my dad,
Both so proud
But I was not

Later that day I thought about my performance
And why I wasn't proud.
Then I remembered, I wanted another part
But I hadn't worked hard enough.
'So that is why I wasn't proud'
Said I, without realising that one day
I would become a *super star!*

Cordelia Scott (11)
Cator Park School For Girls

Animals

Animals big, animals small,
Animals soft, animals cool.
Animals friendly, animals scary,
Whatever animal, save them all!

Animals wild, animals scared,
Animals nice, animals rule.
Animals hairy, animals bendy,
But all the animals are one family.

Melanie Nagle (13)
Cator Park School For Girls

What Is Winter?

What is winter?
Winter is a time for fun and games
Little children cheering because
Santa is near.
As the snow drops and little noses
And cheeks go rosy red,
As the day is ending, little ones look out
Of the window before bed.
They wake up in the night and hear
Hooves tapping on the roofs.
They run to the window, faces
Filled with happiness as they see
Santa ride away.
He shouts, 'Yo-ho-ho! Merry Christmas
And a happy New Year!'

Lisa Wennell (12)
Cator Park School For Girls

My Best Friend

My best friend is very weird,
My best friend has a six foot beard!

My best friend is very funny,
My best friend has a pet bunny.

My best friend loves art,
My best friend does loads of farts!

My best friend is allergic to rain,
My best friend has been to Spain.

My best friend is from outer space,
My best friend like to slap my face!

My best friend is very pretty,
My best friend has raced in the Grand Prix!

Hannah Partington (11)
Cator Park School For Girls

Witch's Brew

Take a pinch of skin
And a few greenflies
Take pus from an ear
And a couple of eyes.

Take hair, so green
And toes, so dead
Take a dead, old hand
And a chopped off head

Take a smelly foot
And some human blood
Take a lightning bolt
About to go thud!

Take a shredded snake
And a dead old rat
Take the nose of a girl
Named, Suzy Pat.

Then mix it up well
Yeah, mix it up good
And top it off with rosy cheeks
And more black hair, hmm well you could!

Then chant these words,
'Kill Jeff! Kill Jeff!
Now chant these words,
'Death, death, death, death!'

Larissa Barnett (11)
Cator Park School For Girls

Love

You watch the news in the evening and see what's going on
Snuggled up to your parents
Their grasp and cuddles strong.
A loved one
To hold you tight and keep you safe from harm.
To guide you on the right path
To lead you by your arm.

I often think of children
Who need a hug or two,
For those who have no parents
Or someone to turn to.
So think yourself lucky
To have someone who loves you,
For when the day comes
You can share your love too.

So when you go to bed tonight
Think of someone who's in need
Who has no hugs and kisses
Or nobody to lead.
So please, everybody
Show some love today
For many have no one to love
Share with, work or play.

Nisa Cooper (13)
Cator Park School For Girls

Autumn Weather

Autumn is here,
Leaves are falling.
Flowers are dying
Autumn is here.
Children are dressing up, shouting in the streets,
Knocking on doors, looking for treats,
Autumn is here.
Bang! The fireworks go in the night sky,
Pretty colours up so very high.
Autumn is here,
Autumn weather's been -
Hallowe'en has gone!
Fireworks disappeared but there is still more to come,
Weather is going to get colder,
Presents will appear
Under the Christmas tree,
Christmas is near!

Sinead Castineira (12)
Cator Park School For Girls

Winter

When I see the big, dark clouds in the morning,
I know it's winter
When I see the snow falling down
I know it's winter
When I need to wrap up warm
I know it's winter
When it's dark really early
I know it's winter
When daytime turns to night
I know it's winter
When I see the Christmas tree sparkly and bright
I know it's winter.

Zoe Williams (12)
Cator Park School For Girls

Take Me Out Of My Shoes

Take me out of my shoes,
The leather is beginning to fade.
The laces are tatty and frayed.

My confidence has gone away,
Because a new girl came in today.
Her hair was pulled up in a bun,
From my mind it took away all of the sun.

Her face shone like a beam of light,
This left me in the corner, full with fright.

My smile has been taken away,
I'm all alone, like a dog that's stray.

The school bell has made its awful sound,
Too late, I've already been pushed to the ground.
My coat is now extremely worn,
My skin is now swollen and torn.

I can feel the blood down my face,
On the floor I feel like a disgrace.
I feel angry, full with rage,
It's like I've been trapped in a prison-like cage.

I went and told the teacher all about it,
Then something inside me lit.
I felt much better and relieved.
I wasn't feeling peeved.

I had let my secret go,
My soul had regained its glow.
From then on I hadn't bled,
And from my life the bully had fled.

Poppy Feakins (12)
Cator Park School For Girls

Train Journey

Bridges, lamp posts whizzing by
Cars and traffic roads
Birds perched on rooftops
Lorries with different loads
Litter, graffiti everywhere
People rushing around
Going round the recycling centre
And I can't hear a sound!

The humming of the train and the noise in the carriage
Train going round like the beat of thumping Garage
People eating fish and chips and jogging in the park
Birds were singing sweetly but daytime is fading now.
It's getting kind of dark.

Funfairs going round. School children hip
Children shouting and saying, 'Can you skip?'
Teenager planting gum behind his ear
Pretty girl getting into tizzy
Trains going faster, getting dizzy!

A tramp looks rustic in his tattered shoes
Carrying his small plastic bags
And eating a Mars bar, savouring every bit
Wearing dog-eared rags.

School children bouncing balls
Businessmen walking
Man sorting out his tools
Tall office blocks
A mum talking,
It's a pleasant sunny day.

A voice on the train echoes for a while
The day has come to a halt
I sit there, staring and smile
Train getting slower
Oh, it's stopped! Kids run off
Leaving cats, they've dropped.

Johanna Francois-Walcott (12)
Cator Park School For Girls

Look Mummy What A Beautiful Sight We See

As the night approaches and
The weather is getting colder,
As the spiders hide away and the
Little children are in their bed,
As the snow falls down onto the
Spider's webs, they glisten like
Shimmering diamonds, beautifully in
The corner of the shed.
'Look Mummy, what a beautiful sight we see'
As the morning approaches and
The children look out to see their
Tiny little faces light up with glee.
'Look Mummy, what a beautiful sight we see'
As the colours rise in the world, the
Children are astonished and say . . .
'Look Mummy, what a beautiful sight we see.'

Bianca Denise Forde (12)
Cator Park School For Girls

The Alley Man

Every day after school I see a strange looking man
Walking up and down the alley.
He has strange eyes
Like he is blind.
He has a grey T-shirt and it's all holey
And his trousers are all torn.
He wears a cap with a huge slit on the side.
He has this huge scar down his face.
I try not to let it scare me.
He looks about 20 but he has grey hair
So I don't know what age he is.

Sarah Cullen (14)
Cator Park School For Girls

Winter Season

The corner of my eye
 Catches a glimpse,.
I turn around to look
The Christmas tree glints.
The birch tree leaves are
Covered in snow, I walk
Underneath, it drip-drops on the
Tip of my nose.
In the corner of the garden
Against the fence stands a
Spider's web, dragging its
Raindrops, ready to fall!
Fireworks start and make the day glow,
All the different colours,
Make me want to glow.
Children are out and about
Making snowmen and having
Snow fights, they put huge
Smiles on the snowman's face
Christmas carols can be heard
I could sit here all night and
Listen to their sweet angel voices.
Merry Christmas!

Alda Krasniqi (12)
Cator Park School For Girls

Winter Season

Cold breeze
Leaves are falling
Here comes a new
Season coming

Slippery, shiny ice
You could go skating in
White snow
Even whiter than white.

Brown trees
They look like bony knees
They're just brown sticks
With curvy flicks

There we go
It's the winter season,
Now it's time to think about
What presents you're
Going to be given
And shout with glee.

Tammika West (12)
Cator Park School For Girls

Am I?

Am I looking
Or am I dreaming?
Am I touching
Or am I dreaming?
Am I feeling
Or am I dreaming?
Am I right
Or am I wrong?
People say yes
People say no,
All I can say
Is what I know.

Kylie Graham (15)
Cator Park School For Girls

Hallowe'en

Danger, danger, Hallowe'en is near
Danger, danger, Hallowe'en is here
It's near, it's here
The full moon is here.
It's time for the werewolf to appear
So it's time for us to be aware!

Danger, danger Hallowe'en is near
Danger, danger, Hallowe'en is here
It's now time for the tricksters to appear.

With candy here and candy there
There's a little candy in the air.
Slow and calm it's now one o'clock
All street lights are out

Danger, danger, Hallowe'en is here,
So we'd better be aware!

It's time, it's time,
It's Hallowe'en time.
Danger, danger, Hallowe'en's here.

Acacia Northe (12)
Cator Park School For Girls

Recipe For A Doctor

Stir a box full of white overalls
Pour a glassful of blood
Take a pinch of patients
And peel a fresh bit of skin
And add some eyeballs,
A pinch of equipment and medicines
Heat a bit of hair
And mix all together to make a doctor!

Anna-Louise Johnson (11)
Cator Park School For Girls

Own Mind

Why can't you say your mind
that's what it's there for.
When badness is what you find
then you'll say no more.

Other's minds are not yours.
Why don't you take a stand
cos when you start breaking laws
you'll have no place to land.

It doesn't make you dumb.
It doesn't make you sad
it just makes you someone -
that isn't turning bad.

If you look into yourself
then you will find
just that something else
with its own mind.

Abisola Akinbowale (14)
Cator Park School For Girls

The Hottest Day Of Summer

It's a hot day today, everyone is having fun
What shall we do? What shall we do? It's a hot day today!
The sun's burning bright, the water is splashing.
What shall we do? What shall we do? It's a hot day today
The flowers are swishing from side to side
What shall we do? What shall we do? It's a hot day today
We could go swimming or play in the park.
What shall we do? What shall we do? It's a hot day today
Shall we have a water fight or get a suntan?
What shall we do? What shall we do? It's a hot day today.
Sunbathe as long as you can till we find something to do,
What shall we do? What shall we do? It's a hot day today.
Please help us, please help us to find something to do today.
What shall we do? What shall we do? It's a sunny day today.

Kelisha Vincent (12)
Cator Park School For Girls

Life And Lifelessness

Life begins in mere seconds, the process speeding along.
Life is a calm Utopia of the mind, nine months of security
and gradual development.
Life is shown in a new light, torn away from serenity and peace of
mind, into panic, blurs of strange alien figures, a familiar signal from
one of the alien faces brings calm.
Life is strange and an unusual thing, so much is ahead as time passes
Life is full of pain and work, struggles and triumphs,
it is becoming difficult.
Life is full of pressure and high expectations, disappointments
and hardships, life is difficult.
Life is full of abandonment, independence, debt and
back-breaking work - life is lonely!
Life has meaning, when two halves of the same whole come together
and are joined in an almost unbreakable bond,
life is full of headaches and warmth.
Life has firsts and memorable experiences reflecting on your own
at one time, life is full of pride and happiness.
Lifelessness draws near, life is now a painful struggle of endless
torment, life is full of endlessness.
Lifelessness will come soon but there are still moments worth
waiting for, life is full of new generations.
Lifelessness has come, it was worth living to see it, life is full
of unforgettable experiences.
Life is over, it takes mere seconds, the process comes to an end,
life is complete.

Monique Tulloch (12)
Cator Park School For Girls

Inside Out . . .

Inside out is what it's all about,
Outside in ain't nothing but a thing.
White, black, purple or blue.
Does colour really mean anything to you?
I think everyone needs to stop the fight,
As we're all the same colour when you turn off the light.
Sexy, buff, cute or sweet.
Are you looking for a trick or a treat?
Ugly, standard, butters or nice,
Do you really know me? You better think twice.
Is the problem it's just the outside you see?
You never know I might be a junkie or have an old STD.
But then I could be the best
The most valuable prize you could ever invest,
Or really you could be looking at my bumper or my chest.
Cos when you look at that you probably forget about the rest.
Don't worry I'm not just talking about sex,
As you know I don't want to get the parentals vexed.
Look at the world today and you will see,
How much people are hating on 'we'
If we cast each other as one.
And if we could all just get along
Also if in ourselves we had a little less doubt
We could judge each other from the *inside out.*

Kloé Dean (14)
Cator Park School For Girls

Suicidal

They say not to take your life,
But they don't know, they haven't got a clue,
They don't know what it feels like when people
Say the world would be a better place without you,
Yes it's true.
You could have killed me and I could have got a degree,
Now I'm stuck with you, and I got bare hatred,
Up inside of me.
Wanting to do this since Year 4,
Now the years have gone on, and I want to do it even more,
It's like, you think you're hot, even though I think I'm not,
Or, you're a slut, a hoe, wind up in bed with a friend, a foe.
You think I'm dumb, always out to get some,
You don't trust me, no privacy.
What's gonna happen in the end?
Dead silence, bullet in the head,
Train tracks splattered.

Now gone to a better place where people love you
And you get to say grace
I'm gone
It's over
Six foot under.

Chelaine Young (15)
Cator Park School For Girls

That Faraway Land

The best time of day is night,
To close your eyes
It feels just right.
To let your sorrows drown away,
To prepare you for another hard day.
Your mind takes you
To a faraway land
Where white and black
Smile and stand
Happy together
Hand in hand.
This land is full of love and care,
Why can't I really be there!
I wake in the morning feeling great!
But I wasn't to know
It was a mistake
Walking to school
That very same day,
Cheery and happy
Smiling away.
A few seconds later
I was really hurt
They treated me
Like a piece of dirt!
Why couldn't I be in . . .
That faraway land
Smiling with friends
Hand in hand.

Victoria Studd (14)
Cator Park School For Girls

Friendship

Friendship cannot be bought or sold,
It can only be earned to hold,
Trust is one of the important things,
That makes two people make a link.

Friends are angels from above,
Sent by God for me to love,
So if you're down and upset too,
Just remember I'm here for you.

Tiny stars shining bright,
It's time for me to say goodnight,
So close your eyes and snuggle up tight,
It's time for me to say goodnight.

Sleeping's not a fashion, friendship's not a trend,
Friendship is for me and you my friend,
Friends are important, friendship's not a game,
I really hope we will always stay the same.

Of all the friends I've ever met,
You're the one I won't forget,
And if I die before you do,
I'll go to Heaven and wait for you.

I'll give the angels back their wings,
And risk the loss of everything,
Just to prove my friendship is true,
I'm thankful to have friends like you.

Nabisa Sulaiman (14)
Cator Park School For Girls

Irresistible

The rumble inside me
Sends me to open the door
I've been so good
But I can't resist anymore.

It's just laying there
Like it's not doing anything wrong
I can't cope anymore
It has been too long.

My hand reaches out
I can't stop anymore
I take a huge bite
And close the fridge door.

I close my eyes
And in it goes
Then the sensations
Start to arose.

The moment it was over
And it was all gone
I knew straight away
That I had done wrong.

Someone had got back
Going to see what I'd done
So I hid all the evidence
And started to run.

Only one thing left to say
Will it stay, or come out the other way?
Never again will I go that far
But maybe tomorrow only half a choco bar!

Katie Eastop (14)
Cator Park School For Girls

Aware?

You may have a tough head
Greasy hair or think
What the heck, who cares
People do judge
So you think,
I'd better be aware.

So you slick up your hair
Now look like a sket
Now do you think, what the heck?

You've become something you're not
You've changed your attitude towards work,
Teachers - are you aware?
What you eat,
What you wear,
Your family,
Start to be aware.

In the outside world you're stylish,
Thinking how neeky was I!

But now you're with your new crowd
Smoking God knows what
Thinking will I live or could I die?

People may class you as:
Neeky
Too smart
Or you'll never fit in
But remember
It's what you are inside
Smart, fat or thin.

Rhetorical question -
Are you *aware*?

Marsha Gayle (15)
Cator Park School For Girls

Only You Can Save Yourself

They tease, they hurt,
They treat you like dirt.

They get you in trouble,
You're all in a muddle.

No one saves you,
What are you gonna do?

They're there again in your face,
You pick up the pace.

They follow you still,
They won't go away.

Where's your knight in shining armour,
There isn't a knight.

Only you can save yourself.

Kaylie Rule (14)
Cator Park School For Girls

What One?

Do you pick and choose your friends?
If you do it will never end!
Do you like them thin, fat, tall or small?
I must admit I don't mind at all!

Once you've found your friend,
Never let go or it will end!
I've found my friend, and what a great feeling it is!
For it's not everyday
That friendship can be found.

What a special friend I have indeed
Whom I will always need -
I think the world of you and I'm glad to know,
The friendship will always glow.

Grace Pepper (14)
Cator Park School For Girls

Daddy's Girl

One little girl stood in the crowd,
Waiting for her daddy's name to be read out loud.

When nothing came she started to cry,
As now she knew her daddy had died.

She tried to think positive but she already knew,
The fire had burned her daddy too.

There were millions or cries in her ears,
But she didn't make a noise, her eyes were just full of tears.

Her mum's eyes were exactly the same,
There was a puddle of tears settled next to the drain.

Her arms were now clutched around her baby girl,
She was twisting all her delicate curls.

She said, 'Don't worry, everything will be OK.'
As she turned her daughter around and walked away.

That poor little girl she was only ten,
When she saw her innocent daddy's life come to an end.

Rachel Fryer (14)
Cator Park School For Girls

How To Make A Monster

Drop in five cat hairs
Grate in the claw of a crocodile.
Boil for a minute.
Crack in two bear eyes.
Cut four worms and add their heads,
Mix well three times.
Slip in six rabbits ears.
Put in the juice of an orange.
Drizzle in the slime of a slug.
Leave to set overnight
And in the morning rising out of the pot
Will be a monster.

Robyn Burge (11)
Cator Park School For Girls

Do You Wish?

Do you sometimes wish
You were somebody other than you?
Do you sometimes wish
You could do other than what you do?
I want to be someone
Other than me.
I want to be able
To see the sun through the trees.
I want to see the birds
On their maiden flight.
I want to see
The creatures of the night,
Like will-'o-the-wisp
And wolves' eyes that gleam
But I live in the city
Not in my dreams.

Yolanda Shaw (14)
Cator Park School For Girls

Stop Living In The Past

You say that we are racist,
I'm not saying you're wrong or right,
But you have gained so much over the years,
You have a place to stay at night.

You were beaten and treated like slaves,
But that's all history,
Times have changed, just look and see,
Nowadays it's a different society.

This is how I see it, equal!
You've got some rights at last,
But you're always talking about the olden days,
Look forward, stop living in the past!

Lynsey Steedman (14)
Cator Park School For Girls

The Golden Gleaming Face

The sun is a giant smiling face
A golden person looking down
She casts upon us her shining rays
But never seems to give a frown.

Her gleaming appearance brightens the world
As she ventures across the sky
Her look is always bleachy blonde
As she and the clouds drift by.

The sun is a golden bird
A yellow ball or badge
She is a glorious circular star
Because of the smile she has.

She brightens the world in the morning
When her features begin to rise
But as she fades in the evening
Is a time humans must despise.

The sun is a giant smiling face
As beautiful as can be
As she looks down on the Earth
Her kindness we can see.

Jayde Balderston (11)
Chatham Grammar School For Girls

One

One wish is what you get,
What do you wish for?
1000 wishes doesn't count,
Would you wish for destiny to be shown before us?
Would you wish to be famous?
Would you wish for world peace?
People never think,
If we put our minds together,
All our wishes can come true.

Jennifer Shannon (13)
Chatham Grammar School For Girls

Think Before You Act

An empty page,
A blank canvas,
A similarity.

A black hole,
A blue sky,
A difference.

A crossword,
A wordsearch,
A puzzle.

A human?
An alien?
A question?

The answer -
Everyone and everything has its own personality,
So think before you act.

Stephanie Shaw (12)
Chatham Grammar School For Girls

Fire

Dancing flames skipping around the sky.
Smoke chewing at our eyes.
The wood running away from the fire,
The fire laughing, knowing it can't get away.
The smoke joking with the fire.
Finally it cripples the wood
And starts grinding its razor-sharp teeth.
The fire paces up and down limply,
Searching for fuel,
Swearing and shaking fists,
It dies and smoulders.

Rebecca Reay (12)
Chatham Grammar School For Girls

I Hate To Love You

I hate the way you smile at me,
I hate the way you stare,
I hate those big Doc Marten boots
And trashy clothes you wear.

I hate the way you clasp your hands,
The way you stomp your feet,
I hate the way you stand and sit,
I hate the way you eat.

I hate the way you always care,
The way you understand,
I hate the electricity I get,
Whenever you touch my hand.

I hate it when you have to leave,
You never say goodbye,
I hate the things you say to me
And how they make me cry.

But most of all, what I hate the most,
But you will never know,
I hate the fact I care for you,
And that I love you so.

Angela Davey (13)
Chatham Grammar School For Girls

Cat

As I walked through the door,
I saw a cat eating chocolate galore!
I said to the stranger, who sat near the seat
'How can you eat, eat and eat?'
'Well,' it started to speak,
'The reason I eat, eat and eat,
Is because I'm an eating forever cat,
Which means I eat forever until there is no more days left in a year.'
And this cat was crystal clear.
Then me and this cat sat down and talked,
But after a while this cat looked down and squawked.
'What's wrong?' I cried
'I've run out of chocolate, I'm going to die.'
'I've got no chocolate,' I said to the cat,
'But I've got healthy food, try that.'
The cat looked confused but said, 'Okay, I'll try,'
So I gave him some carrot and lentil pie,
Some cous cous, peas, green beans and corn.
The cat scoffed it down, then said with a yawn,
'That is the best meal I have had in my life,
It's better than chocolate, that's just trouble and strife.
I am tired now after such a fine meal
I think I'll retire now, but I'll cut you a deal.
If you provide my food every day from now on
I'll give you £10 a week until my fat is all gone.'
So we shook hands and parted, after making amends,
And ever since then we have been greatest of friends!

Emily Henderson (12)
Chatham Grammar School For Girls

A Shy Person's Wishes

With the relaxing sound of waves moving,
On a calm and peaceful day, listen . . . silence,
With the golden sand trickling through my toes,
With the sun shining on the ripples of the sea,
There, I wish, I would much rather be.
Deep in the marshland where no one will find me,
With greens and browns, and peculiar, unusual sounds,
With animals no one has even seen.
With now, green blankets of fresh cut grass,
With things that are timid, and shy and free,
Wishing to be;
With candyfloss clouds in the sapphire sky,
With polar bears skating on the freezing ice,
Discovering the isolated desert,
Scorching hot, purple, pink skies and sound free,
With things that are rooted, and firm and deep,
Quiet to lie, and dreamless to sleep,
With showers of rain sprinkling the newborn flowers,
With cotton wool lambs springing from place to place,
With freshly scented meadows, all yellow bright,
With trees rustling, whispering, talking at night,
Whistling wind crying through the window cracks,
A vibrant breeze swaying the old trees,
Gliding like a mermaid through the deepest ocean,
Splashing like the dolphin diving deep again,
Sending Morse code ripples for a thousand miles,
Maybe high in the sky, looking, listening,
With care to find our world such a beautiful place,
Anywhere, anywhere, out of this forlorn, awful spell.

Emma Richards (13)
Chatham Grammar School For Girls

Me

I'm a dove, flying through the trees
All of a sudden I come back to the real world
All I am is a homeless teenager
I'm free
I stumble to my feet gathering my things
I'm ready for the next doorway.

I'm a hunted animal. A sleazy, greasy dosser
I remain anonymous
Nobody knows who I am
I'm only a sleazy, greasy dosser
So show me the next doorway.

Nobody cares who I am
Everybody looks and stares
I eat the crumbs everybody drops!
I wish I was flying through the stars
I'm only a sleazy, greasy dosser
After all!

Laura Davies (13)
Christchurch CE High School

Homelessness

H is for hungry with nothing to eat
O is for outgoing with nowhere to stay
M is for murder who kills the trash
E is for empty heart
L is for a little boy who's all alone
E is for eager to find somewhere to stay
S is for silly leaving your home
S is for smelly rain-soaked bed
N is for naughty boy of them all
E is for easy done
S is for scared boy
S is for scanky bed.

Jay Sage (14)
Christchurch CE High School

Piece Of Dirt

There I am every day
Scared!
My toes freezing
Fingertips numb
Everyone walking by
Wearing
Coats
Scarves
Hats.

I think to myself that was
Me once upon a time . . .
I wish sometimes people walk by
And spare me money
They think I spend it on booze
But I need clothes . . .
I walk down streets
People behind whispering
'Skank'
I lay down wishing
I could stop the world and start my life again
With Mum, Dad . . .
But I am a piece of dirt
When people look at
I say, 'I'll never be like *that!*'

Billy Charles (13)
Christchurch CE High School

Afraid

I am a loving girl
Then my mum turned on me
So homeless I was
Sad and lonely

Nowhere to go
And crying at night, just me on my own
Want to see the world
Want to take a chance on life
So let me go

Scared of my life
Wonder what's around my corner
I just want to feel safe in my own skin
To be happy again

Thinking about what my life used to be like
Nice and calm, and now . . .
Afraid!

Hayley Simmons (13)
Christchurch CE High School

Homelessness

H ungry with nothing to eat
O blivion like me in the street
M ean people to meet
E vil weather as cold as ice
L ost in the snow it's not nice
E xist do I? You have to think twice
S hivering in the snow it's really bad
S now gets deep have to move on that's I had
N o one cares, just walk past and make me sad
E veryone happy but not me
S cared of scruffy scroungers
who take my home when I go for a pee!
S omeone calls me a street rat and greasy,
others say I'm not easy!

Aiesha Carter (13)
Christchurch CE High School

Homelessness

Where my body's so cold
My body so sore
I feel like I'm getting older

So quickly, so fast I feel like I'm dying
And hunger, I ignore
My brain is so ignorant,
I feel like I'm non-existant.

I feel a lot of pain
Because I miss my mum and my sister
I might be dying slowly.

My life is like a broken pencil
There's no point.

Nobody cares about me
I feel like crying . . . but I won't
I will not cry

I have to stay *strong!*

Damion Maskell (13)
Christchurch CE High School

Homelessness

H is for hungry with nothing to eat
O is for out - nowhere to stay
M is for an ugly monster on the street
E is for eating like a hunted animal
L is for little boy
E is for your life exploding
S is for a nice sleep
S is for sleeping bag
N is for numb bum
E is for eternal oblivion
S is for sponger
S is for squatted.

Luke Stonham (13)
Christchurch CE High School

Homeless

That's me
Walking
Down
The street.

Smelly,
Everyone
Ignores
Me

Invisible,
No one
Notices

Empty
But for the
Pain!

They walk past,
Mutter under breath!
'Loser!'

A flame
Going out . . .
Nothing I can do.

Danielle Taylor (14)
Christchurch CE High School

Homeless

Run away from
Home
No place to call
Home
I look like a
Street rat
I came out of the
Tunnel
I feel
Like a hunted animal
My heart feels
Empty
People think we are
Dirty dossers
Dying
On the streets
Of London
There's no place
Like home
I'm getting older
Time goes fast
When you are
Begging for
Money
I'm at the top of
A spiral stairs
I don't know where
I'm going to land
Down!

Danny Bradshaw (13)
Christchurch CE High School

Homeless

I am homeless
I have nothing but a cardboard box . . .

I have no money
People go past me and laugh : . .
Everyone says I am a dirty dosser . . .
I am a street rat. I would love to have a house
And some good food . . .
I sleep down at the railway
Because there are not a lot of people . . .
I don't like begging
Nobody cares about me.
I want to cry but I don't . . .
My life is just a mess.
People go past and say,
'Look at that beggar, he's a tramp!'
Some people give me money so I can get a sandwich . . .
I used to live in a doorway.
I wish I was in a nice house with a big fire . . .
I moved here cos the police
Were going to take me to a hostel
So I moved here in a cardboard box.

Lee Pearce (13)
Christchurch CE High School

Homeless Is Unhappy

Homeless they wait
Homeless they are
Old rags they wear
They freeze in the air!

Shelter they look for
Shelter they hunt for
Shelter they find
Shelter they die for!

Here I am right here
I know you can see me
I can see you
But you walk right past!

Homeless they are, homeless they be
I see they're nobodies!

Barry Blackall (13)
Christchurch CE High School

Lonely

What a sunny morning
Nothing to break the dawning
All the problems in my home
I think I'm better off alone.

I am a street rat
I'm a stray, like a cat
Nowhere to go
I am so low

People talk a lot of trash
They have taken all my cash
I don't know what to do
Who can I talk to?

Maxine Goldsmith (13)
Christchurch CE High School

Homelessness

Homelessness don't sound nice.
Out and about all the time.
Mum - I think about her all the time.
Unless you go home you won't know.
Eating stuff you don't want.
Sleeping in garbage can.
Nightmares every night, what I don't want.
Every night the light goes out of my eyes.
Street rats that's what I feel like.
Sleeping scruffy scrounger . . .
That's what I am.

Stephen Staras (13)
Christchurch CE High School

Beauty

A light bulb in the shape of a beautiful woman called Beauty,
She lies inside every female,
Our bodies are like a piece of black net,
And so the light inside our bodies can sieve through.

Some people don't have Beauty in them,
And so they don't shine nor stand out.
Without Beauty in us, our bodies are hollow and empty.

Some people look attractive,
But without the light from within, they are not beautiful.
Appearance has got nothing to do with Beauty,
It's the light inside that counts.

Tomi Fadoju (12)
Cobham Hall

New Hope

Winter's deathly chill comes crawling,
Bringing an everlasting spiral of doom.
Naked trees with ghost-like figures,
Swaying swiftly in the wind.

Spring arrives; rebirth and growing,
New and old things are remade.
Flowers sprout and climate changes,
Slowly sealing winter's tomb.

Angeliki Kosti (14)
Cobham Hall

The Dentist

As I walk down the street,
I can't help but stare at my feet,
Because off to the dentist's I do go,
Pain is coming, I expect so.

As I sit in the chair,
I can't help but feel quite scared.
As the dentist walks in the door,
I just try to be ignored.

On and on he takes his time,
So I decide to write this rhyme,
Then as he reaches for the drill,
You can believe how I must feel.

For me there is a sudden fear,
As the drill draws nearer and near.
But before I know it, it's all over,
And then I'm back on the streets of Dover.

Oliver Carpenter (14)
Dover Grammar School For Boys

The Poem About You

I stand at the lake
As an old man,
The water ripples and
All that is me has stopped.
My thoughts are all on
You as I see you in the water,
And I think to myself,
What are you in the sky?
Are you a bird
Flying through the wind?
Or are you an angel
In the clouds looking at me?
All I know is that you
Are my angel in my eyes.
I remember the cold, windy
Nights where we would find
Comfort in each other's arms
And happiness would come to me.
I think back to our childhood,
When I first met you,
All people saw it in us,
Love.
You were the one who
Asked to dance,
I'll never forget that night,
You looked like a swan in the moonlight.

And as I kneel down by your grave,
I realise that I am alone.

Connor Lehan-Finn (12)
Dover Grammar School For Boys

World War I

The shells fly and scar the ground,
But still living men can be found,
Fighting and killing,
In the weather that's chilling,
The rank stench of war
And yet no exit through a door,
Men that die,
Just fall on the field and lie,
Injured men shout without a sound,
While others hide behind a mound,
Men of honour, men of valour,
All fight under the same banner,
Artillery fires with a deafening thud,
All goes flying, guts and blood,
The scars of battle dig deep,
Many men in eternal sleep,
Trenches all flooded,
Most men are all bloodied,
The freezing cold around your feet,
In the wind, rain and heavy sleet,
Screams go out,
Battle hangs heavy all about,
The guns stop from the English line,
The officer raises his whistle to sign,
All men over the top,
This is when the soldiers' hearts stop,
The whistle is blown,
The brave men climb over with no ammunition shown,
They walk over no-man's-land,
Not looking back at their trenches, unmanned,
The men that wouldn't go fell to the shot of the officer,
That is why those numbers were of so much lesser,
The machine-guns start to blaze,
The soldiers only see a daze,
This isn't war, this is a slaughter,
What about the man's wife and daughter,
Lions led by donkeys they'd say,
The donkeys had a great price to pay,
The lives of men in 1914-1918,

Were those who saw the worst they'd seen,
Thousands killed day by day
And yet we still feel the consequences today,
Life in the trenches was worse than Hell,
Soldier's sanity bombarded by every shell,
The men that walked over the land,
Had lived in places unfit to be manned,
The soldiers fell line by line
And men still living in the trenches dreaded the sign,
This was war for the unlucky some,
This is a poem on World War I.

Jack Gregory (12)
Dover Grammar School For Boys

Polar Bear

The polar bear hunts its prey
Like a bleached lion in the wilderness.
Its muscular body
Built like a tank and just as unstoppable.
It goes for the kill
As fierce as the British rugby team.
It tears apart its food as easy as bread.
It curls up calmly, like snowfall.

Liam Petch (12)
Dover Grammar School For Boys

Autumn

A utumn is a time of fall,
U ntil it starts to get cool,
T urning to winter it slowly goes,
U se of wool, jumpers are sewn,
M other Nature is so hot and cold,
N othing alike, spring unfolds.

Jeremy Delsignore (12)
Dover Grammar School For Boys

Up In The Hills

Up in the hills where the blackberries grow
The sun shines down and the wind does blow,
The tall trees sway
As the children play
And their voices are heard in the distance.

Up in the hills where the children are,
No sign of a bus or lorry or car,
One child dies
And another one cries,
But no one can hear in the distance.

Up in the hills where the blackberries grow,
The sun shines down and the wind does blow.
The parents fear
As they cannot hear
The children playing in the distance.

Zak Fisher (15)
Dover Grammar School For Boys

The Wind And Rain

The wind howls out of turn,
It howls and scares the little ones till their spines shiver,
It feels like God has coughed or something,
It's scary at night, it seems like a ghost has awoken,
It is as cold as ice or something colder, like the Antarctic.

The rain kind of makes a song when it hits the ground,
It seems that the angels have been crying when it rains,
It is fun splashing about in the puddles,
It is nice when it is hot and it rains and a rainbow appears,
The colours of the rainbow make me wonder, *how did they get there?*

Jared Wills (12)
Dover Grammar School For Boys

Night-Time

When it is night,
The bright sun rotates its way over the sky,
The sparkling moon arises,
When it is night.

When it is night,
A dark evening creeps up,
The sun disappears in a red glow,
When it is night.

After the night,
A clear morning appears,
The white moon fades away,
After the night.

After the night,
The bold moon cannot be seen,
The sun slowly arcs its way over the sky,
After the night.

Benjamin James Curtis (12)
Dover Grammar School For Boys

The Autumn

The autumn draws closer,
The summer is at an end.
Night-time is longer,
Daytime is short.

The crisp, brown leaves
Lying on the ground,
The floor is cold,
No children in the street.

The beggars are cold,
As we are warm.
The autumn draws closer,
Creeping with colours.

Sam Elliott (12)
Dover Grammar School For Boys

The Second World War

T he nights are loud with planes and bombs.
H itler plans to take over the world.
E ach night is too dangerous to go to sleep.

S evere wounds cause people's deaths.
E nemy's planning their next attack.
C hurchill inspires all around.
O n the hills, soldiers hide.
N azi's follow Hitler's every move.
'D ie, Germans, die,' shout the English.

W ill there ever be any peace?
O h God, have pity on us all.
R ely on no one, you don't know who they could be.
L iving is our only hope.
'D addy don't leave,' desperate children shout.

W hite cliffs of Dover is our last chance.
A rmies clash in full-out war.
'R un, run into the bomb shelter,' shout Mums.

Sam Cooke (12)
Dover Grammar School For Boys

The Journey

Setting off early in the morning,
Seeing trees, smelling cabbages, feeling cold.
The steady whirr of wheels on tarmac,
Driving for any age.
Arriving at my destination,
Stepping out onto the damp ground
And breathing the air of a new place,
A new time,
A new adventure
For strangers like me.

Alex Williams (12)
Dover Grammar School For Boys

Ocean Travel

If I could travel
The oceans blue,
These are the things
That I would do:

Fly with puffins
Under the sea.
Dive with seagulls
And have fish for my tea.

Cling to the tail
Of a rolling whale.
Leap with dolphins
In a buffeting gale.

Soar with an eagle,
Hunt with a shark.
Play with the seals,
Then fly home before dark.

Ryan Doble (12)
Dover Grammar School For Boys

The Waves

The waves broke upon the shore as the wind blew my hair,
The waves broke upon the shore as the sun warmed my neck,
The waves broke upon the shore as my children built sandcastles
The waves broke upon the shore as the seagulls glided strong,
The waves broke upon the shore as the pebbles moved beneath
                                                    my feet,
The waves broke upon the shore as I left the beach.

Robert Stewkesbury (12)
Dover Grammar School For Boys

Senses

Taste

T asting all the flavours of the world,
A ll the different flavoured foods,
S eeing all the different types of food,
T elling what things taste like,
E very single day.

Feel

F eeling all the different textures and
E motions inside you.
E very day you feel something different,
L ike happiness or even anger too.

Hear

H earing all the different sounds of the world and
E very single noise.
A nything has a noise,
R eal or not!

See

S eeing all the different things in the world and
E very special sight and
E very tiny speck.

Smell

S mells can either be good or bad,
M aybe sometimes awful,
E ven if it's good,
L ethal or surprising, but everybody
L ikes their own type of smell!

Jake Sandford (12)
Dover Grammar School For Boys

The Old Sailor

The old sailor sailed through the seven seas,
He seemed to be in his early fifties.
He saw nothing except land, sea and air,
His head was becoming cold and bare.
He was bearded grey
And stayed on the boat night and day.
He had no family to comfort him,
His eyesight was becoming short and thin.
The sailor is nearing his end on Earth,
Will he ever reach Australia's Perth?
Land is nearing, will he make it?
Or will he be buried in the underground pit?

Thomas Etheridge (12)
Dover Grammar School For Boys

Place

There's a place I remember faintly,
The image looks sort of painted.
It had a big dome,
Like the ones in Rome.
It had rapids that if you were too small,
Would suck you under like a spinning ball.
It had palm trees inside,
Like the beach or seaside.
It had forest around,
Like the outskirts of a town.
The day I remember the name,
Will be the day I go again!

Nicholas Odell (12)
Dover Grammar School For Boys

My Home

I rewind my thoughts a while back,
To one special day,
When my family and I set off on an adventure,
Set off to our home.
As we stepped outside the plane,
The sun's rays glimmered down on me,
I started to sweat,
I could not breathe because of the humidity,
I started to look around,
I felt like a stranger in my own home,
Like a polar bear in a desert,
Where everything is new to me.
I looked at my parents,
Their faces full of joy,
For they remembered when they were little
And they lived here,
As for my little brother and me,
It was the first time visiting our country! Sudan.
We stayed in Sudan for a month or two,
Visiting families, going out
And I think to myself,
I think I finally belong,
I talk in another language fluently,
Able to communicate with people,
Laughing with them, playing with them,
Finally the day came,
The day I dreaded the most,
It was time to go back to England,
Would my adventure become a memory?
The question remains unanswered.

Moamen Nasr (12)
Dover Grammar School For Boys

A Normal Day At The Office?

Waiting for a taxicab,
On a rather normal day.
Going back to the office
And put my worries at bay.

And yet, as I stand there,
On this, a normal day,
I can't stop thinking,
Of objects far away.

In the cab, the radio,
Tells me of good and crime.
I am already late
And haven't got the time.

The taxi driver,
Goes straight and not around the bend.
Not the side of the office block,
But up to the other end.

'Hey, stop!' I yell,
But the driver's bailed.
The car's not taxed,
So it's getting tailed.

I jumped in the front seat
And then I found,
The taxi had no brakes,
I was dumbfounded!

I jumped out of the window,
Over a bridge,
I almost got sliced,
On a sharp, jagged ridge.

The cops couldn't find me
And I got away.
Did someone try to kill me?
I don't know to this day.

Lewis Hook (12)
Dover Grammar School For Boys

Reflection

I look in the calming water
And
All I see is a rippling face,
I
Think to myself,
What
Could this mean?
I
Think that if my rippling self
Is
A different,
Nicer person than
Me,
He may be let free and I put in his place,
I
Become a dark shadow,
A
Reflection.

Michael Bushe (12)
Dover Grammar School For Boys

Sunset In The Arctic

The bitter wind blowing against my face,
Smelling like pine in the mountains.

The Arctic fox howling at the sunset,
Like a wolf at the moon.

The sun going down in a hurry,
When really there is no reason.

The polar cubs playing in the snow,
As if not a care in the world.

Nicholas Saunders (13)
Dover Grammar School For Boys

My Unlucky Day

Today at school I skipped Latin.
Me and Josh casually chatting,
But then, to my horror, along comes Hainsey!
I started to run, but Josh is big and lazy.
Out of breath, he ground to a halt.
The teacher's eyes like a thousand volts.
So Josh got caught and taken to the office,
He's rubbish at skiving, only a novice.
What should I do? I thought to myself,
This hard situation requires some stealth.
So down the deserted corridor I crept,
Past the staffroom where the teachers slept
And there it was, where I wanted to go
A little bit risky, yes I know.
I plucked up my courage and took a deep breath,
But suddenly the door opened, bang on my head.
I suppose I'm lucky that I'm not dead
And I'm only lying on a medical room bed.
If I stay here I'm sure to get done
And from past experience, that is no fun,
So I planned my escape and headed for the door,
The pain in my head I tried to ignore.
The way to freedom was just down here,
Away from the teachers and the growing fear,
Knowing my luck, something was more than sure to happen
And there was a prefect waiting for escapees and ready to catch 'em.
There goes my lunch break and after school.
Now I wish I hadn't been such a fool,
But do not worry, I will prevail,
There is always next lesson and then I won't fail!

Daniel Allen (13)
Dover Grammar School For Boys

October

October
Chilly
Thrashing winds
Overnight coldness
Brown, dying plants
Ebbing leaves
Remembrance.

Leslie Hayden (12)
Dover Grammar School For Boys

One In Every Class

She's the girl,
The one over there,
With the spot-free face
And the glossy brown hair.

The teacher's pet,
Who can do no wrong,
Gets on well with teachers,
But here, she doesn't belong.

The loser,
The one all alone,
She wants to make friends,
To them, she is not known.

The class clown,
Whose jokes never end,
People only laugh,
Because they want to be her friend.

Then this other girl,
Who is very friendly
And likes to have fun,
She is . . . me!

Hannah Wales (14)
Dover Grammar School For Girls

Scars

The pain was immense,
The pain was tremendous,
The blood trickled
Down my arm,
Scars, don't hurt.

The blood congealed,
Over the pain,
But it still hurt,
The scab flaked off,
Scars, don't hurt.

All that is left,
Is the scar,
It brings tears to my eyes,
It makes me cry,
Scars, hurt.

Sinead Chapman (12)
Dover Grammar School For Girls

Dancing

As I put on my dancing shoes,
My feet know what they've got to do.
They first go left and then go right,
They want to dance with all their might.
I start to get the beat by clapping,
Then my feet join in with tapping.
Now I think I've got the beat,
I can jump and stomp my feet.
There's no stopping me dancing,
I am all leaping and prancing.
My dance skirt is twirling,
I am turning and whirling.
The teacher suddenly says to stop,
I stop, take a drink and flop.
I really like my lesson in dance
And can't wait for another chance.

Emily Turner (13)
Dover Grammar School For Girls

Paintbox

(About moving from Australia to England)

I'm losing my colour,
I'm not me anymore,
My background's slowly fading,
Fading into one
And all my colour's gone.

In my picture the sun's not burning,
The colour's mixing into grey
And my colour's changing,
My tan's going, no longer there
And all my colour's gone.

Now in my picture, the old characters have gone
And new ones shall replace them,
My accent's slowly changing,
I'm not me anymore
And all my colour's gone.

Every picture I look at,
Is changing every time.
Where's the picture I used to know?
I've left it far behind.
Is all my colour gone?

My colour is slowly changing,
But my paintbox will stay the same.

Abigail Hall & Jenny Lovell (12)
Dover Grammar School For Girls

Bad Dreams

I lie in bed, each and every night,
Wondering what bad dreams I'll have tonight?
Last night my dream made me shudder with fright,
A mummy came creeping up on me,
Told me not to worry,
But I did.
It scared me,
It did,
I nearly screamed the house right down.
My mum came running in.
He said, 'My coffin awaits me yet,'
This mummy I wish I'd never met.
Will this happen again tonight?
It's too late I hear,
It's too late I fear,
Because the mummy is coming near.

Samantha Sheppard (11)
Dover Grammar School For Girls

The Sickly Sweet Shop

Doom! Doom! The stopped clock strikes midnight,
Things start to move in the half-light.
Shadowy shapes of long dead children,
Reaching for sweets, mouldy and rotten.

Gummy snakes like writhing maggots in despair;
Tattered cobwebs hanging down the creaking stair;
Pattering rats' feet on the dusty, disused till;
Ghostly laughter from mouths that can never be still.

Decaying jelly babies in their glass coffin,
Musty odours of skeletons long forgotten.
The sweet stench of death is all around,
Willing us to join them, underground.

Jennifer Ashcroft (12)
Dover Grammar School For Girls

Starting Secondary

St Mary's days are far behind,
They'll always be with me in my mind.
New challenges ahead at DGGS,
More work? More homework? You ask, and yes.
It's harder than we are used to,
But with hard work, we'll all get through.
Doing the homework can be a drag,
So is carrying a heavy bag.
I like the school as there are no boys,
Their noise and mess, it just annoys.
There's a place for them to go to too,
Perhaps it is the local zoo.

New friends, some bright and some dizzy,
New topics to learn, all keep us busy.
We've lots to learn, more each day,
I feel at home in 7J.

I'd say to all that feel quite wary,
Come to the Grammar, it's not that scary.
The school seems big, the kids do too,
But ask yourself, what shall I do,
Go elsewhere? - That's second best,
Come to DGGS, forget the rest.

Charlotte Hyde (12)
Dover Grammar School For Girls

A Love For A Horse

Sleek and slender striding forward,
Strong and reliably relaxed across the line,
Another win for the nation's favourite, never cutting it fine.

Steady talons ready to race,
Her beautiful fur wrapped up her grace,
Never with a hair out of place, a winner like her,
Nobody wanted to face.

Her name was Breeze,
If all of her rosettes cover her up,
They would flow down to her knees,
She was a white pure bred Arab, which had a steady pace.

Then in the worlds longest race, Breeze was up ready to come
Face to face,
She ran so fast everyone was proud,
A mile to the finish line, a gasp went through the crowd.

Breeze was down, she had tripped quite badly,
Her talon was ripped and so seriously swelling,
The jockey was shocked and had fallen loudly,
But Breeze was up and off without no telling.

Her heart said go, the pain said no.

She made it first to the finish line
And looked at me without a sound,
With one sad little look, she collapsed to the floor, I ran for the door.

I ran out of the stadium and onto the pitch,
Where somebody was treating her, my jockey Mitch,
My poor little mare had passed away from me, but at least now
She was free.

The funeral was finished as they buried poor Breeze,
I blew her one final kiss and I set off, tears creeping on my knees.
On top of her grave was carved a white dove,
Bearing the words, I died with love.

Sophie Biot (12)
Dover Grammar School For Girls

Hope

Looking out of that window,
The sky is painted grey,
Looking over the rooftops
And the young children play.

Inside me is all darkness,
The same to match the sky,
I feel as if I'm slipping away,
To just fall and fall into a dark pit.

The darkness wraps around me,
Like a sausage in a roll,
My mind has gone completely blank,
As if someone has switched it off.

I feel as if this unhappiness will never, never end,
That I'm trapped here like a prisoner,
Trapped forever,
Never able to go on.

But then, a beam of light,
As thin as a sewing thread,
My heart blossoms like spring flowers,
Warmth spreads down to my fingertips and toes.

A rush of confused joy flows through my head,
It's getting lighter,
The darkness fades away
And a light bulb turns on in my head.

Now I'm looking out of that window,
The sky is painted with more colours than I can count,
Looking over the rooftops
And the young children play.

Anne Plumridge (13)
Dover Grammar School For Girls

Discrimination

Black, white, blue or green,
Why don't we live together? Listen to what I mean.
Why put up with discrimination?
They put our brothers and sisters through alienation.

Hindu or Jewish, why is there hate?
Why did apartheid segregate?
Why can't we all come together and sing?
Why did someone shoot Martin Luther King?

Qu'ran or the Bible, does it matter what we read?
Why can't people just take heed?
Different religions and different beliefs,
Why do bullies put us through this grief?

Should it matter, our race or size?
So when will everyone realise,
That what holy book we read or what skin we're in,
Means nothing, compared to what's within?

Black, white, blue or green,
Why don't we live together? Listen to what I mean.
Why put up with discrimination?
They put our brothers and sisters through alienation.

Rachel Gisby (13)
Dover Grammar School For Girls

What Is A Poem?

Painting pictures,
In your head,
Always using words instead,
The paintbrush left far behind,
Now it's time to open the mind.

Ryanne Robertson (11)
Dover Grammar School For Girls

Evacuee

As I sit and stare,
and watch the flashing glare
of buildings, cars and trams,
together we sit all crammed.

Fields flashing by,
as I try not to cry.
The train is slowing though,
where I am I do not know.

A lady grabs my arm,
I sort of feel a bit alarmed.
She reads my tag,
and takes my bag.

Then she moans in a stern voice,
'Be good or else you'll have no choice.'
A cold sweat is running down my face,
like coming last in a race.

Catherine Watts (11)
Dover Grammar School For Girls

Marriage

She used to make me feel so free, young and light,
But now she just makes me angry with all her weeping day and night.
People might say I should love her, no matter what
But when she talks, it is all nonsense to me because
                                        she ends up weeping.
Why do I have to bear this infuriating behaviour all the time
When my fuse is burning out inch by inch each day?
And soon I will be gone
And she will be weeping evermore
Making a flood over my grave!

Georgia Beverton (12)
Dover Grammar School For Girls

The Spring

Buds appear on the bare trees,
New life begins every day,
The winter brought the cold wind's breezes
The spring brought the singing queen of May.

The young lambs bleat,
And the foals, they neigh,
Fox cubs eat meat,
And are happy and gay.

Little mice try to stand,
But they stumble and trip,
Little ducks rest on the sand,
As they take a long kip.

The plants grow anew,
And the dewdrops are clear,
The tulips are blue,
And the wildlife is so near.

The newborn chicks cheep,
As their eggs do hatch,
The small badgers creep,
As they make for their first catch.

Foxgloves glint pink,
In the bright sun ray,
Roses are red,
On this hot, sunny day.

Young calves stand on knobbly knees,
As the piglets lie in the hay,
The winter brought the cold wind's breeze,
The spring brought the singing queen of May.

Robin Dyer (12)
Dover Grammar School For Girls

Spring's Bounties

Spring is . . .
A field of golden daffodils, dancing in the gentle breeze,
as yellow as the sun itself.
Blossom swirling,
drifting to the ground making a thin carpet,
too delicate to touch.
Newborn lambs frolicking in the grassy fields,
going nowhere in particular, trying to get to the rainbow's end.
A sea of green replacing the grey of cold.
The warmth gradually seeping through the harsh winter season,
like many flowers opening their glorious heads ready to astonish
the world with their beauty.
Bees ready to be busy, visiting each flower in turn,
like a cheery neighbour coming to offer their greetings.
The climax of the year, when all is well with the world.
This season is the greatest, the best!
This season is the best . . .

Racheal Haddon (12)
Dover Grammar School For Girls

My Mum

My mum's the brightest star,
Also the best mum by far.
She's the best smelling rose you'll ever find,
You will always hear her in my mind.
My heart will continue to love her much more,
She will always make me feel better when I'm sore.
Mummy, I will continue to love you more and more.

Now we are apart,
It is breaking my heart,
Now we're not together,
You taught me how to be clever,
Just like you.
I can hear you calling me Lozzy McGoo.
We are sad to see you go,
We're all feeling rather low,
But Mummy I will continue to love you more and more.

Loren Selby (11)
Dover Grammar School For Girls

Winter Mouse

Winter mouse, better scuttle home
it's getting cold now and this is when the foxes roam.
Winter mouse, in the frosty field
go to your house where the warmth is a shield.
Winter mouse, it's getting late
run faster to your tiny wooden gate.
Winter mouse, it's starting to snow
the sun is rising, the moon, getting low.
Winter mouse, finally in the warm
escaping the snowy swirling storm.
Winter mouse by the fire aglow
what you dream of I wish to know.
Winter mouse in your patchwork bed
adventures flying through your head.
Winter mouse, snuggle deep
have a long, peaceful sleep.
Winter mouse, it's very late
when will the storm's noises ever abate?
Winter mouse, the sun is out
it's time for you to skip and shout.
Winter mouse, the storm's at an end
no need to worry, my little furry friend.

Georgia Broadhurst (11)
Dover Grammar School For Girls

Marriage

At first pure bliss,
Oh no, what is this?
My temper is rising
I can't help despising
That wife of mine.

I hate seeing her tears
She's drowning in fears
They call me a bully
I can't understand fully
That wife of mine.

I come across tough
I love to play rough
It's just so easy
To make her feel queasy
That wife of mine

One day I'll beat her
And really defeat her
One day I will tell
What if I go to Hell?
That wife of mine

Then they'll see
How nice I can be
And act all sorry
I'm without a worry
Without that wife of mine

Amber Tonkin (12)
Dover Grammar School For Girls

Well, okay, maybe not
I realised that I forgot
I love her really you see
That's how nice I can be
That wife of mine.

I'll love her to my dying day
Or not, who can say?
Wherever she goes I'll be there
To give her a little scare
That wife of mine.

Time's fading fast
Our love cannot last
In Heaven or Hell
All I will tell
To that wife of mine.

It came sooner that you'd think
I had more than one drink
Our love came to an end,
She drove me round the bend
That wife of mine.

I really regret it
I shouldn't have meant it
Now, well, she's dead as can be
Dead, dead, dead like me
That wife of mine!

Happy Days

When I was your age,
Birthdays were just a cake,
Tea at five,
What you were given, you ate.
Milkmen and greengrocers
Delivered every day,
Coal fires lit in every room
And houses never locked all day.
Sixpences in the Christmas pudding,
I wanted to be the first,
A bottle of milk at school
To quench my thirst.
Black and white TV and radiograms,
No videos or PCs to play,
A picnic on a bike ride,
We played with friends all day.
Clothes were passed from brothers to sisters,
But Sunday you wore your best.
Chips in newspaper and peas from a tin,
You shared it with the rest.

Louisa Love (12)
Dover Grammar School For Girls

And I'm Left Alone

Love is a complicated thing,
My marriage has gone down the drain,
My wife just cries,
My child just runs
And I'm left alone!

My wife used to go out dancing,
But that was not to last,
My child was so active,
But now he sits down all day
And I am left alone!

I try to keep the family going,
It's very hard to do,
When I want to hug my child,
He goes and hides away
And I'm left alone!

I'm getting old,
My wife is too,
But when she dies,
I will too,
So I'm not alone!

Katy Spice (12)
Dover Grammar School For Girls

When I Was Young

You eat your TV dinner
Whilst watching a DVD,
When I was small TVs were rare
And we ate with the family,
We went to church, took long walks
We had little but didn't care.

You play your CDs; send a text
Whilst wearing designer shoes,
In my day conversations took place
And our clothes we did not choose,
We did chores - pocket money was earned,
Life was simple; it was not a race.

You sulk and swear and answer back,
Instructions you ignore,
When I was young we showed respect
And we did not slam the door!
Time moves on, life quickly changes
One day you will also reflect.

Fay Goddard (12)
Dover Grammar School For Girls

At The Seaside

At Deal seafront there is a pier,
Sometimes the sea is rough, sometimes it's clear,
The stones are sometimes smooth,
When the sea hits the shore they move,
At Dover docks,
The sea hits the rocks,
On the sea I saw a ship,
Just as I was having a dip,
I can grab
A crab,
I am on a boat,
It can float,
And I eat my prawns,
As a lovely day dawns,
In the sea fish sail,
I can hear a whale,
In the seashells I can hear the sea roar,
When the sea hits the shore,
When I count to three,
I will be in the sea.

Sian Smith (11)
Dover Grammar School For Girls

The Flower

The marriage was born,
Like a beautiful white flower,
Dawning,
Dawning.

It was bright and colourful,
Like the young couple's love for each other.

It stayed like this for months,
Standing there,
Proud and strong.

Autumn came . . .

The couple started to drift apart,
Their love for each other was going.
Petal by petal,
Leaf by leaf,
Hanging,
Limp as a piece of string.

The flower is now dead,
It looks back at its younger years in sorrow,
As it sees the last of its petals
Dragged away in the wind.

Jessica Capon (12)
Dover Grammar School For Girls

Afraid

In the darkest corner of my heart
Hidden, protected, unknown
Are these memories I've locked up
For so long, forgotten.

It's time to open the box
To remember what I've tried to forget
Voices, tears, images and scars
Are now on full show.

I am a new creation
I have a new life
I started over not so long ago
But I still can't let go.

My tears are those of blood
My heart has been slashed again
There are too many scars
I'm broken once more.

I'm too scared to forget
It's too late again
I want to be with God
I don't want to be afraid anymore . . .

Lisa Mannings (14)
Dover Grammar School For Girls

You Think . . .

'You think you'll live forever,
Nothing can hurt you
Damage your lungs and liver,
With drink and drugs too.'
'Yeah, yeah, Mum.'

'You think money grows on trees,
No need to get a job,
Mum and Dad will pay your fees,
You're acting like a slob!'
'Yeah, yeah, Mum.'

'You think you should come first,
No time for Ps and Qs
No time to help the aged -
It's them that you accuse.'
'Sorry, Mum, I love you!'

Iona Joy McCarvill (12)
Dover Grammar School For Girls

Winter

Along with winter comes
the soft white snow.
Along with winter comes
the chilly breeze
Along with winter out come
the woolly hats and jackets
so we don't freeze.

James Liam Taylor (11)
Hartsdown Technology College

A Letter To God

Dear God,

Thank you for birds and trees
Thank you for busy bees
Thank you for waterfalls
Thank you for swimming pools
Thank you for Dad and Mum
Thank you for the burning sun

Thank you for Harry Potter
Thank you for terracotta
Thank you for sandy beaches
Thank you for my teachers

Thank you for cats and dogs
Thank you for muddy hogs
Thank you for the moon and stars
Thank you for Earth and Mars

Thank you for Free Willy
Thank you for my cat, Tilly

Thank you for tides and waves
Thank you for scary caves

Thank you for you and me
Thank you for the things we see

Yours faithfully,
Mary

Mary Elizabeth Bull (11)
Hartsdown Technology College

I Am

I am funny and weird
I wonder if there is a ghost
I hear a little whisper in my ear
I see something floating around
I want to meet a ghost
I am funny and weird

I pretend to be a ghost
I feel one go past me
I worry what happens to them
I cry when they don't like me
I am funny and weird

I know they exist
I say they're my friends
I dream about them whisking me away
I try to make people know them
I hope they live happily ever after
I am funny and weird.

Emma Palmer (11)
Hartsdown Technology College

My Friend And I

This poem is about a friend and me,
Climbing up and down a tree.
I can see you helping me,
Climbing up this big, big tree.

Now it's my turn to help you,
You help me and I help you.
You took some conkers off the tree,
You gave half to you and half to me.

You went home and so did I,
You fell and started to cry.
I helped you up and said 'Goodbye.'
I saw my friend and I said, 'Hi.'

Abbie Jayne Morrison (11)
Hartsdown Technology College

I Am

I am a 'Caring Comic' who likes cats
I wonder how the world really began
I hear bells ringing in a deep, dark sea
I see a bird with my cat in the garden sipping tea
I want to be a 'Caring King' who likes cats
I am a 'Caring Comic' who likes cats

I pretend that I am a famous wrestler
I feel the clouds beneath my feet lifting me higher
I touch the stars and moon in the deep, dark night
I worry that friends get bullied in a fight
I cry for the child more unfortunate than me
I am a 'Caring King' who likes cats

I know that war is now a part of life
I say that every picture tells a story
I dream of being a millionaire
I try to be a good son for my parents to be proud of
I hope for my parents to have a long and happy life
I am a 'Caring Comic' who likes cats.

Mark Blake (11)
Hartsdown Technology College

Wintertime

It's wintertime once again
It's getting very cold and we wrap up warm
It's wintertime once again
It's snowing very hard
It's wintertime once again
It rains an awful lot
But it's nearly Christmas time again.

Sophie Scargill (12)
Hartsdown Technology College

I Am

I am a mad, mad girl who loves monkeys,
I wonder if I could swing from tree to tree?
I hear the sound of the jungle,
I see my mates hiding with me,
I am a mad, mad girl who loves monkeys.

I pretend I am an orang-utan,
I feel I need to eat bananas and hang
When I touch the vines and swing.
I worry my friend's in trouble,
I cry when I am alone,
I am a mad, mad girl who loves monkeys.

I know you may think I'm stupid,
I say, 'I am who I am.'
I dream of a life in the wild,
I try not to be too alone,
I hope one day I'll be famous,
I am a mad, mad girl who loves monkeys.

Imogen Culliford-Morcom (11)
Hartsdown Technology College

Friends

My friends are a loony lot, they always jump and shout
They always try to annoy each other when we're out and about.

There's Charlotte, who's popular especially with the boys,
Then there's Ella, who would rather play with toys.
There's Lucy, Emily, Holly, Sarah, Kirsty too,
Grant, Daniel, Jordan, Tom, Graeme and Ollie too,
They all went to Cliftonville and I still see them now!

There's Fairlie who's a troublemaker,
Sarah is a pain too!

Are they always like this . . .? Well, maybe!

Samantha Evans (11)
Hartsdown Technology College

My Mates

My mate Rachael is loads of fun
But sometimes she annoys everyone.

My mate Jade is a crazy girl
Sometimes she gets us all in a whirl.

My mate Tash loves her hair
She wears it the same everywhere.

My mate Becky is so tall
I can't imagine her very small.

My mate Natalie is really sweet
She does not like to eat meat.

My mate Alice loves football
Sometimes she's as comforting as a brick wall.

My mate Tayla is sometimes mad
And sometimes she is sad.

Nadia Kerrigan (13)
Hartsdown Technology College

My Nan

I miss you so much,
I wish you were here,
I remember the good times we had,
And I remember so sad,
Losing you was the worst thing that ever happened to me,
I wish I could sit down with you and have a cup of tea,
When I was little I dreamed that I could come round
                         your house and see you on my own,
But now you're gone, I can't do that,
I think about you all time and I still think about the
                               great times we had.

Chanelle Smethers (12)
Hartsdown Technology College

Out For The Count

He is in the dressing room away from the crowd,
He wants to win so that he can be crowned.

He puts on his gloves and his bandages too,
Before he goes on, he nips to the loo,
The MC announces he is on his way,
The boxing match has been dubbed 'Judgement Day'!
They're in the ring, they both touch gloves,
They are both wearing white and move like two doves,
The bell is struck once,
It's the start of round one,
They both throw jabs but most are blocked,
It's the end of the round and they both are stopped,
They come from the corners and come out fighting,
One falls to the floor and loses his sighting,
He's on the floor and out for the count,
Everyone cheers when they hear the ref shout!

George Flegg (13)
Hartsdown Technology College

The War

I was in the Second World War,
When everything was full of gore,
When I thought I was ignored,
I was pulled to the floor,
My friend saw a bullet coming towards me,
When suddenly I see the army flee,
We ran after them,
When I saw a bomb under my feet,
I retreated,
When I saw my friends being blown to pieces,
All I could find of them were their dog tags,
So I relieved myself with a fag.

Chris Tazey (12)
Hartsdown Technology College

The West

In the west,
You have to be the best.
You're going to have to last
Or you will be put in the past.

Bang! Goes the gun.
Lots of people run.
Everyone's silent
Or otherwise violent.

Some people covered in blood
Lying in the mud.
People trying to be nice
But shot like mice.

People say,
'I will win some day.'

But will they?

Tom Solly (13)
Hartsdown Technology College

Sam

There was a boy called Sam,
Who like eating Spam,
He played football,
In the school hall,
He got a detention,
That he didn't mention.

He told his mum,
Who smacked his bum,
And that was the end of Sam,
Who liked eating Spam.

Nathan Smith (12)
Hartsdown Technology College

Blue

Blue is a colour,
Blue is the colour of my bedroom,
That makes you gleam and shine.
Blue's my favourite colour,
And, boy, is it bright?
Blue's the colour of the sea,
Blue is the colour of Chelsea,
That makes you jump for joy.

Abbie Bridson (12)
Hartsdown Technology College

Brothers

B rothers are so irritating
R ight pain in the neck.
O h why did they have to be my brothers?
T ough luck for me.
H aving them every day
E ven at school
R eally, my brother's not so bad, at least he's not my
S ister!

Terry Peake (11)
Hartsdown Technology College

Food

Food is great
Food is the best
Pizza is nice
And so is ice cream,
Jelly is cool,
Curry is hot,
Food is the best, no matter what!

Gareth Mason (11)
Hartsdown Technology College

Lost

As I paddle through the sea,
I pull up the line,
All the fish flee,
I know I won't survive . . .

As I search for land,
I know I'm definitely lost,
This trip was not planned,
I shiver in the frost.

I'm dripping wet and freezing cold,
I hear the bombs dropping near,
But I must be big and bold,
Nobody will realise my fear.

As I see a boat far ahead,
I panic and scream,
Many tears I shed,
I wish it was all a dream . . .

Levi Baker (13)
Hartsdown Technology College

Nan, The Hole In My Heart

This is my heart and there is a hole,
Your face I cannot see,
Your hands I cannot touch,
I miss you so much,
But that's how it's got to be.
I see you in my head,
I see you in my dreams,
I'll see you in my eyes for real
When we meet again.
Rest peacefully, Nan.

Lauren Miller (12)
Hartsdown Technology College

Fireworks

Fireworks go *bang*
Fireworks go *boom*
In every direction
They zoom, zoom, zoom!

They split into the air
Like a flash of light
They're heard around the world
In the dead of night

Catherine wheels
Go round and round
Sparks shoot off
And fall to the ground

The fireworks are over
Gone for this year
If you did not make it
Next year make sure you're here!

Eleanor Katherine Thain (11)
Hartsdown Technology College

Christmas

Christmas is a time to celebrate the birth of Jesus,
Christmas is a festival celebrated by Christians,
Christmas is a time to be with our families.

Christmas is a time to unwrap presents,
Christmas is a time to eat a big roast dinner,
Christmas is a time to pull a cracker.

Christmas is a time to build a snowman,
Christmas is a time to decorate the Christmas tree,
Christmas is a time to listen to the church bells ring out loud!

Megan Sara Brackenborough (11)
Hartsdown Technology College

A Regretful Soldier

Horror, tension, is what we feel,
As to stop the evil, we have to kill,
There are so many lives to save,
We have to help and be brave.

Bang! Bang! Another dead!
We watch on as they drop their heads
But they will be pushed to one side,
Nothing more said.

Regret is what I feel now,
As I kill one more,
I'm evil, I'm bad
I'm making people ever so sad!

Benjamin Whisson (13)
Hartsdown Technology College

My Dog

I had a dog,
He was very bright,
Although he couldn't
Talk, read and write.

Now my dog
He was very special,
He could sleep like a log
Or play when he wanted.

Yeah my dog was cool
He was the best
And he wouldn't follow
A single rule!

Kier Buchanan-Cox (11)
Hartsdown Technology College

Me

Here I am, standing here,
No one else to stand and sneer
I don't care what people think
They can think whatever,
It won't hurt me not now, or ever.

Look at me, ooh yippee!
What am I proud of? It's only me.
Everyone's special in their own way,
But I have something special.
I won't tell, no way!

Do you want to know? Do you want to know?
Well, tough, it's mine.
It's mine, mine, mine!
Oh! I have to go, I have to go,
See you in a mo, see you in a mo!

Toni Paul (11)
Hartsdown Technology College

Christmas Day

I woke up on Christmas Day
And got out of my bed.
I went downstairs and opened the door
And I saw a good moped.

I was very pleased
That I had a moped,
So I went back upstairs
And went back to bed.

Robert Adrian Watts
Hartsdown Technology College

The Footy Match

Before the match the fans are excited
With their friends they are united
Down the pub they have a drink
Have a laugh and start to think

Then off to the ground the fans go
Always happy, never low
They cheer their team to the bitter end
Even if they lose, their spirits will always mend

Then one touch of sheer class
A great long, searching pass
And he's through, on goal he must score
But, alas, it goes wide and the fans roar

The final whistle goes and it's all over
Margate lose 3-0 to Dover
The fans are angry; full of rage
But next week will start with a brand new page.

Mark Baker (13)
Hartsdown Technology College

Manchester United

Sir Alex encourages them
They take centre once again
Nistelrooy shoots
And scores a goal

Giggsy crosses
Scholesy headers it in again
Silvestre takes, kicks it wide

The match finishes
2-0 yet again.

Ricky Lee Lambert (11)
Hartsdown Technology College

My Hamster, Harvey . . .

My hamster, Harvey,
Is small and fat.
He has brown fur,
And doesn't get on with the cat.

He sleeps all day,
And eats all night,
He is friendly,
Fat but light.

When he escapes,
He is fast on his feet,
Lucky the cat hasn't
Had him for meat!

I love my hamster,
He is lovely,
Really sweet
And really bubbly!

Rachael Barker (13)
Hartsdown Technology College

Friends

A friend is someone who's there for you,
No matter what you've been through.
They'll always be by your side,
The only person who's really kind.
They'll have some good sides,
And some bad sides,
But will always show their good side.
They will always make you laugh,
And they will feel like your other half.
A friend is all you need.

Abby Aldous (13)
Hartsdown Technology College

What Is War?

What is war? Is it good
Or is it like starving without food?
Guns are shooting, the world is shaken
Just like a frying pan full of bacon

Blood and guts everywhere
No one else would bother to care
Innocent people are dying
Victorious opposition is lying

Family members full of shock
Who were then hit with a wooden block
Saddam Hussein, a dictator of war
Now has become very poor.

War is over, we all are excited
Dictator of war never again to be sighted!

Ben Akhurst (13)
Hartsdown Technology College

Someone

Someone somewhere
Dreams of your smile
And why they are dreaming
No life is worthwhile
So if you are lonely
Remember it's true
I am that someone
Who's dreaming of you
I think of you
I dream of you
Nothing can stop me
I am crazy about you!

Rochene Turney (13)
Hartsdown Technology College

My New Sister

Mum shouts, my sister screams
Dad's got that look on his face that always means,
'Go to your room and don't come back down,
wipe that smirk off your face, stop acting like a clown.'
Five seconds later I am up in my room
thinking to myself, *I'll go down soon.*
Ten minutes later I'm in the same spot
then I hear silence, the screaming has stopped.

I go down the stairs, creak,
and then I see my sister asleep.
As soon as she looks up, she starts off again
and screams like she is in so much pain.
Mum comes in, angry and red
and then she shouts 'I thought you were in bed!'
Dad opens the front door and looks inside.
'What have I done now?' I could have cried.
I ran upstairs and crying fell to the ground,
nothing is the same now my sister's around!

Rhiannon Ayles (13)
Hartsdown Technology College

My Friend

My friend Taya is lots of fun
She is friends with everyone.

She loves to lie in the sun
While eating an iced bun.

She is also very sweet
She's the friend you would like to meet.

She is very nice
And is as cool as ice.

Alice Freeman (13)
Hartsdown Technology College

I Hate School

You get up for school every day,
All work, no play.
Wearing uniform everyone hates,
Or falling out with your mates.
I'm always in trouble,
For having a fight or blowing a bubble.
Watching time pass,
Moving around, class to class.
The teachers are all the same,
Standing around calling your name.
As the day goes on forever,
You don't feel very clever.
Staring at a board or book,
Making charts or even cook.
Staring at the ceiling can't teach you much,
When instructions are given, I swear they're in Dutch!
IT and history,
Spanish and geography.
All these lessons we have to take,
Catching up in lunch or break.
Sitting on those uncomfortable chairs,
All your classmates giving you glares.
We are forced to go,
Why can't we say 'No!'
Seeing teachers after school,
Standing around, you feel a fool.
Detentions are so boring,
Just sitting there snoring.
I'm not bullied or feeling sad,
I just hate school, it drives me mad.

Portia Godden (13)
Hartsdown Technology College

The Pain I Felt That Day

Why so much hurt, why so much pain?
It scars your life so badly, words can't even explain.
How can you tell people what you have seen or done?
The memories are too painful to talk about for fun.
Some of the things I have seen, still keep me up at night.
I lie there in my bed, completely frozen in my mind,
Until it is finally light.

Being a soldier meant everything, the praise and love
I would receive.
Pride, love and happiness are the things I would retrieve.
The weapons were awful, all the guns and knives,
For once I was important, for once in my life.
Killing people was the cowards' way out,
But still I did not understand what war was really all about.

I remember how depressed I was, all sad and cold,
It seems like long ago, now I am old.
There are people all around me, as far as the eye can see
But I realise now that is the loneliest place to be.
I am in a place where no one knows my name, and
I am feeling all alone,
All I have wanted to do for years is go to the place I call home.

Now I am waiting to die, and there is not much I can say,
But I will never forget, for as long as I live,
The pain I felt that day.

Natalie Orr (13)
Hartsdown Technology College

Poem On Love

Being in love is one of those things that no one can explain
Once you're in love and you're sure of it, nothing remains the same
They're the only thing you can think about every day and night
You can't bear to be apart so you never let them out of your sight.

You think they're the one
But not knowing whether they have done
Something to hurt you
Or something to lose you

But you keep it to yourself
It's like waiting on a shelf
Hoping to keep them
For as long as you want them

But if you find they don't want you by their side anymore
And you try and find a cure
Because you never want to part
With something you always cherish in your heart

Being in love is one of those things that no one can explain
Once you're in love and you're sure of it, nothing remains the same
They're the only thing you can think about every day and night
You can't bear to be apart so you never let them out of your sight.

Emilie Arnold (13)
Hartsdown Technology College

His Love Forever

In a house all cold and lonely,
All forlorn and looking bony,
An old man, of the past he thinks.
Like a rotten fish that really stinks,
Could never be alive again
'Til she comes home and maybe then.
He remembers her standing there,
Very pretty with long, dark hair,
Her dress red, clad with white lace,
He has never forgotten her embrace.
He wanted forever for his love to last,
But this really is the past.
And now he sits all cold and alone,
And soon he will be only bone,
When all his life has rotted away,
But in spirit they'll be together, someday!

Carina Banham (14)
Hartsdown Technology College

A Second Lady

He leaned forward to look at her,
Eyes closed shut, ruby red lips and a pale face,
And long, dark hair, black as night,
She lay there, full of grace.
Exhausted she must be
After all her hard work, and then a race
All for his second beauty, second lady,
A baby child
More beautiful than a flower, softer than silk,
More baroque than lace.
Together they lay, side by side, his beloved wife and blessed child
Fresh-faced as they slept and dreamt
Both in their place,
At home.

Ysabelle Bradshaw (13)
Hartsdown Technology College

The World

Have you ever stopped and stared?
Stopped and let the world we share,
Revolve around us as we see,
Death, destruction and a world full of greed?

There's no one to shield me,
No one there to blindfold me from what I see,
Hating, crying, jealousy, dying,
Hurting, lust, love, trust!

With war and hatred flying in the air,
I feel it in the pit of my stomach,
I wish the world would just give in,
I wish the world would just *stop!*

Ella Chapman (13)
Hartsdown Technology College

The One I'll Always Fancy

Her eyes so bright.
Her hair so light.
When she smiles her teeth go shiny
Which makes me think, *oh cor blimey!*
When she puts her hand in the air
All I can do is sit and stare!

Aaron Barnes (14)
Helen Allison School

Dancing

I like dancing
To the music that I pick
I think dancing keeps me fit
That is why I love it!

Marc Fosker (13)
Helen Allison School

All Hail The Simpsons

'Laughter is the best medicine,' as they say
For there is a family of five that make anyone's day
There is a man with two hairs who works at SNPP
There is a fourth-grader who has fun with glee
There is a saxophone player who does not eat meat
There is an untalkative baby who has trouble using her feet
There is a woman whose tall hairstyle is blue
And the thing about their neighbours being religious is true
This family of five has a dog and a cat
The dog is brown and the cat is black like a bat
The woman of the family does not have a job
But to tell the truth, she would never rob!
She did once, however, sell real estate
And her husband has fun to make a debate
The fourth-grader's favourite TV star is a clown
Who is very funny and is never let down
The sax player is a fan of this jazzman
Who does play good music to heat up the pan
And the baby of the family is rather calm
And to tell the truth, she would never harm!

Richard Langworthy (16)
Helen Allison School

The Spot

The spot, the spot
Worse than a blood clot!
Full of pus
But don't make a fuss
If you squeeze too much, it will go like mush
You're probably going through a lot of stress
When it bursts
Don't make a mess
I know when you get scared you get hot
But whatever you are, beware of the spot!

Tony Field (14)
Helen Allison School

Rugby

I like rugby
It stops me
Getting chubby.
On Saturdays
I watch the game
I take my dad
Which is a shame.
When we win
We make a din
We scream and shout
And charge about.
Then home we go
With Dad in tow
Home to Mum
And no more fun.

Ben Hawkes (12)
Helen Allison School

A Bat In My Hat

There was a bat in my hat.
He was as ugly as a rat.
Then I knew what to do
To get rid of him once and for all.
I took him in the hat to the park,
Walking slowly through the dark.
I lifted the hat as the wind blew.
Up and up, the bat flew.
He flew up, up, up into the night,
Heading into the bright moonlight.
He was gone, never to be seen again!

Michael Hines (13)
Helen Allison School

Football

I want to play football sometimes
I'd like to be in goal
I'd kick the ball across the pitch
Football is my soul

Manchester United is my favourite team
I've watched them play at home
Red's my favourite colour
Their kit I'd like to own.

David Wilson (16)
Helen Allison School

Pets

Cats purring
Lying still
Watching birds
From the window sill

Rats' tails
Thin and long
Dragging behind them
All day long.

Dogs barking
As cars run by
Up the cat goes
Towards the sky

Fish swimming
Around and around
In their fish tanks
They make no sound.

All kinds of hamsters
Running on their wheels
Round and round they go
Making little grunts and squeals.

Sarah Dryden (13)
Herne Bay High School

Eden

Only two people on the Earth,
These two people to make birth.

Flowers dancing in the breeze,
Branches of the swaying trees.

The treetops nearly touching the sky,
All the branches reaching high.

Animals everywhere around the place,
Using up the beautiful space.

Colours scattered everywhere,
The rich colours filling the air.

Full of peace and freedom,
Of course this is the garden of *Eden!*

Lauren Hammill (12)
Herne Bay High School

Bonfire

Bonfire Night comes
every November
and it's bound
to light up the sky.

All the rainbow colours
go up with a bang
and everyone goes
'Ooh!' and 'Ahh!'

And as the end comes
everyone goes home
and the fireworks
go to bed for another year.

Craig Ellis (12)
Herne Bay High School

My Pet!

I have a very special pet
He's the cleverest budgie I've ever met!
His cage is all scattered with colourful toys
He's happiest when he's making a noise
He wakes in the morning and rings his bell
He wants to come out, I know, I can tell
He sits on my shoulder and says his name
He flies to the floor, he wants a game
He pushes his ball all over the floor
I get out his trolley so he can some more
His helicopter is his favourite toy
He says, 'Hello Joey' and 'Pretty boy'
He calls the cat and says my name
He sits on your finger, he's very tame
I cover him up as I put him away
I walk slowly and quietly out of the door
He whistles at me and I say,
'*Shh*, Joey no more!'

Natalie Leonard (11)
Herne Bay High School

My Poem

Richard Burns, Richard Burns burning down the track,
Richard Burns, Richard Burns around the corner he learns
Richard Burns, Richard Burns returns on the track.
Richard Burns, Richard Burns turns on tarmac.
Richard Burns, Richard Burns

Britain's best rally driver.

Thomas Robbins (11)
Herne Bay High School

My First Day At School

My first day at school, *wow!*
How did I get here, how?
Who put me here, who?
My mum, that's who. She's the best.

The other children, they're so big
And I feel so small.
I miss my mum, she said it would be fun.
I hope she's right.

I'm walking into the hall.
I wish I could curl up in a ball,
The hall is so big, ever so big
And I'm ever so small.

The day went great,
I got my first merit, hooray!
My mum's ever so pleased with me.
I even learnt some French, *'Qui, qui!'*

I got my first piece of homework, hooray!
What a great day!
I'm ever so pleased I've come here,
Art's the best, I even drew a big bear!

Kelly Gillett (11)
Herne Bay High School

In The Country

In the country everything is silent
Birds chirp, trees rustle
The wind blows slowly through
The stars are shining in the night sky.
The moon appears slowly in the dark sky.

Leanne Greene (11)
Herne Bay High School

My Poem

January, the snow is here,
Everyone's in their duvets, wrapped up nice and warm

February, everyone's out to play,
Playing in the park, everyone's having a laugh

March, everyone's at school and work,
Trying hard at doing work

April is Easter time,
Everyone's eating Easter eggs

May, everyone's having fun
Playing with their friends

June, the sun is out,
Sunbathing on the beach

July, everyone's out on the deckchairs
Licking ice creams

August, people playing in the sea,
Children building sandcastles

September, children are back to school
In their nice new uniforms

October, ghosts and ghouls are about for Hallowe'en,
Bring orange pumpkins

November, remember, remember the 5th of November,
Fire works set off like Guy Fawkes

December, it's Christmas time,
Little ones waiting for Santa.

Sophie Willway (12)
Herne Bay High School

I Am

I am good-looking but sometimes sad.
I wonder if we will land on Mars.
I hear someone cry.
I see dragons.
I want a jet ski.
I am good-looking but sometimes sad.
I pretend I am a stuntman.
I feel a unicorn's horn.
I touch a dragon's tail.
I worry about my dad.
I cry about my dad.
I am good-looking but sometimes sad.
I know that my brother loves a girl.
I am an agnostic.
I dream about wars.
I try to do good work.
I hope I will be rich.
I am good-looking but sometimes sad.

Ben Ashby (11)
Herne Bay High School

Lovesick

When I came to Briary
I was set a curse
In this curse I had an admirer
When I saw her my heart just burst
In my heart there's a hole only she can fill
Her hair is silky as a flower
Her eyes are like the sea
Her glasses are what attract me
But her love is getting weaker
And I hope we can still be friends
Only time will tell!

Adam Winton (11)
Herne Bay High School

I Am

I am lazy but helpful.
I wonder if people will live on different planets.
I hear myself dreaming.
I see my nan in the garden because she has gone to Heaven.
I want to be very good at the guitar.
I sometimes pretend I type quickly on the computer.
I sometimes feel a cold coming on.
I sometimes feel like jumping off a building.
I worry my sister might get picked on at school.

Daniel Lane (11)
Herne Bay High School

Hell!

The darkness, the dampness
The scary chilling rankness
The smell of Hell!
The forever ringing of the bell
The squealing half-dead rats
The evil-looking bats.

Scary though it was,
Nothing compared with being
Stung by 100,000 wasps.

Karma Sharland (13)
Herne Bay High School

The Murder

The mysterious stranger in the shadows.
The fat police without a clue.
A killer with blood on his hands.
The victim's face, pale, and eyes, dark blue.
A person unaware, walking on the sand.
A bloody knife with a stain.
His bloodthirsty bulldog growling.

Joshua Hollands (13)
Herne Bay High School

My World

When I'm older I want to bungee jump out of an aeroplane
and land in a chocolate town, in the future.

In a beautiful dreamy world of mine,
a million stars I shall catch in my palms.

Wish a wish and it all comes true,
stardust, fairy spells, only magic.
I holdout my hand and catch it all.

I find myself falling, falling, where I do not know.
Tiny lights all around me flicker and fly.

Tricks with my eyes I see, I feel,
but do I feel right? Do I see wrong?

Where am I? What am I? I don't know anymore
trapped in this world of mysterious things.

Can't I just fly back home where I belong . . . ?

Kizzy Wildish (11)
Herne Bay High School

Notting Hill Gate Carnival

The sweet scent of the Caribbean food
Tropical music makes me sway to the beat
Laughter and happiness encourages me to dance to my free will.
Shimmering elegant costumes dazzle in the crowded streets.
Extraordinary people with the unique style.
A never-ending party that sticks in the memory!

Eleashia McKenzie (11)
Herne Bay High School

My First Day At School

I walk into school,
I feel like a fool,
Everyone is looking at me,
As I stand by the willow tree.

I don't know where to go,
I am walking very, very slow,
Into my tutor room,
Which seems like a room of doom.

There are words I have never heard before,
As I walk into my English room door,
I look up at the board,
There are horrible-looking words like 'sword'.

We put the date into our books,
We have to write words like 'cooks',
We've now finished the lesson
And we have to write our most favourite possession.

That was my first day at school,
And I can only remember one rule,
Yes, I know that's bad,
But I have to get out of school
Otherwise I will go *mad!*

Gemma Louise Snapes (12)
Herne Bay High School

Dolphins

My dream is to go on a wonderful and exciting ride,
The fast swimmer hitting the water,
The dolphin's long and slippery body,
It's sharp-sided fins,
The wide V-shaped tail,
The dolphin's fine and pointed head,
Its sorry, wide eyes just staring at you as you go by.

Holly Howlett (11)
Herne Bay High School

First Day At School

I went to school one day
It was in September, not June or May.
There were loads of kids
Having pens with lids
Then throwing them all away.

I went to lunch
Having a munch
I had to pay
With these big kids in my way
Giving me a punch!

So although it's been two weeks long
I would still rather go to Hong Kong
And after that
I'll buy a cat!

Kimberley Dancer (11)
Herne Bay High School

My First Day At School

First day at school, where should I go?
There are too many people, too many toes.
When's the bell going to go?
I'll get lost in this toss.

'Boys and girls,' my headmaster will say,
'Welcome to Herne Bay High School today.'
I found my class in the end,
Someone told me I had gone round the wrong bend.

It's almost time to go home,
I've made friends, no longer alone.
The bell goes, here I go through the gate,
Now I can tell my mum it was great!

Megan Bridge (11)
Herne Bay High School

First Day At School

I am worried sick,
I am sitting in the car on the way to school.
My new school!
My tie is strangling me,
My shirt is itching me,
And my shoes are rubbing me!
Not a good start is it?
I wish I was at my old school.

I get out of the car,
My knees are shaking so much
I think I am going to fall over.
When I get to school things aren't so bad
I actually have fun
And guess what?
I don't want to be at my old school.
I want to be at this school!

Amy Rowbotham (11)
Herne Bay High School

First Day At School

A thousand miles from home,
The school is so big,
I don't know what's gonna happen,
I'm scared and frightened too.

Help! Help! A year ten's approaching,
He comes up to me and shakes my hand,
He says 'Good luck' and walks away,
That makes me feel ten times better.

The bell has gone, what do I do?
Waiting for ages, seems like a year,
It's all worth it, I have Mr Findley,
I've got English next.

Michael Dryden (11)
Herne Bay High School

My First Day At Herne Bay High

My first day at Herne Bay High,
Looking up at everyone,
Looking for my friends,
Looking for some teacher to tell me when school ends.

Ring! Ring! The bell goes,
We're rushed into the hall,
Hearing a voice, don't know who it is,
Everyone's looking up, it's the head of the year.

We're called up into our tutor groups,
Waiting for ages, seems like a year,
Finally I am called, I have Mr Robson,
I am one of the lucky ones.

Ean Flood (11)
Herne Bay High School

My First Day At School

The other children are so tall,
It's like talking to a wall,
I'm sure the teacher's wearing a wig,
I think I saw her outside with a cig.

I wish I knew the way,
I'll do anything, even pay,
I think I'll follow my friend
Oh no! Which bend?

The bell's gone, it's time for lunch,
I'll ask to sit with that bunch,
I think I'll give my hair a comb,
Hooray! It's time for home!

Bonita Werner (11)
Herne Bay High School

First Day At School

Ding-dong! School has started,
Where should I go?
Is there anyone here that I know?
Chloe, Jazmin, Katie, Reece, Tom or Joe?

Ring! Ring! The bell has rung,
They're all so tall
And I am so small.
Ring! Ring! The bell has rung,
My life story has just begun!

'In, in!' the teacher screams,
'Get in the hall and on these beams,
And then you're going to get into teams
'In, in!' the teacher screams.
'Get out your pencil case, you have homework.'

Ding-a-ling-ling! It's three o'clock,
Time to go home and get in the flocks
Feed those pigs and do all the housework,
And I'll tell you one thing, I am a jerk
For believing all of those rumours
Because really Herne Bay High School is great!

Rebecca Miller (11)
Herne Bay High School

Missy The Dog

You have smooth fluffy fur
And a short curly tail
You have tall pointy ears
And bright gleaming eyes
You have amazing sharp hearing
And the most excellent sight
You have a very rough bark
And you're the best!

Alex Hogbin (11)
Herne Bay High School

Teachers, Teachers

Teachers, teachers
They babble on all day
Teachers, teachers
They make you work all day.

Teachers, teachers
Sitting there all day
Teachers, teachers
Wishing the time away.

Teachers, teachers,
The bell has gone
Teachers, teachers
The work should be done.

Teachers, teachers
I really think they're creatures
Teachers, teachers,
But really they're just here to teach us.

Joel Borstlap (11)
Herne Bay High School

Satan

The burnt red skin
The pointy long ears
The sharpest nose ever
The dagger-like horns
The fire of Hell

The gates are opening
The urge to kill
The swaying pointy tail
The scariest mask ever

The evil has arisen!

Harry Robertson (11)
Herne Bay High School

The Night Bus

A derelict bus station stands alone,
A wreck of a bus waits to roam.
The passengers, goblins, ghosts and ghouls,
Await to scare the human fools.

The phantom driver goes clickety-click,
Issuing tickets nice and quick.
As the bus starts to run,
Bats and rats follow for fun.

Witches shriek across the sky,
Sniffing vampires wait and sigh.
The destination is ahead,
Will they stay hungry or fully fed?

The silent wheels halt to a stop,
They have arrived at the shop.
Is it Safeway, Asda or Tesco?
No, it's Coronation Street's Frescos!

Joshua Goldsmith (11)
Herne Bay High School

Cars, Cars, Cars!

Start up the car
rev it up
clutch down
turbo on
fly away
mate in
chat a bit
same again
fly away
black windows wound down
turbo up
not being very careful!

Sam Taylor (11)
Herne Bay High School

Bubbles

Bubbles, bubbles, everywhere.
Floating in the park.
All the bubbles in the air.
All around.
There they go.

Blue dancing in the air.
Green spinning round and round.
Red bobbing up and down.
They are so colourful.

Silver has just popped.
Why do they pop?
Orange is gliding through the air.

Purple and green are racing each other.
Purple takes the lead
And is just floating
Off into the distance.

Tasmin Goddard (11)
Herne Bay High School

Independence

Eardrum-piercing air raid sirens
Whilst watching a heart-wrenching death,
Cold and extremely lonely streets
The bloody shooting across the river
Massive gleaming tanks.
Fiery-symbolised missiles killing my friends,
Fighter planes soaring high in the sky
Dreaded silence across the land
Suicidal terrorist killing for no reason.
The brave soldiers on my side
Fighting for me and my country
And our independence.

David Catterick (11)
Herne Bay High School

Tiger, Tiger

Tiger, tiger, standing there,
With your orange and black hair.

Tiger, tiger, standing there,
With your big glimmering teeth.

Tiger, tiger, standing there,
With your big sharp claws.

Tiger, tiger, standing there,
With your fine long tail.

Tiger, tiger, over there,
Dancing on the stage,
You bit your master on the neck,
And now he is in care.

Sarah Styles (11)
Herne Bay High School

My Ghost Poem

Eerie is the slight night,
heart racing and mind wondering
whether to fight or take flight.
The spirits are all around me,
they astound me,
all shapes and sizes I can see,
will they just let me be?
My steps are getting wider and faster,
if I'm not careful I will need a plaster,
the sweat is pouring from my face,
as I see yet another ghoul's face.
Phantoms spin within the air,
suddenly I awake and I'm in my chair!

Ben Sargeant (12)
Herne Bay High School

My Two Cats

I have two cats
They love a pat
Sol is very friendly
Poppy is very shy
I don't know why.

We have to feed them every day
Afterwards they love to play.
They run around the garden a lot.
They've made it a habit
To chase the rabbit.

At night when it's dark
They come in from the park
They come upstairs
To go to bed
To rest their heads.

Jordan Alice Westbury (11)
Herne Bay High School

The Devil

His dark horns poking people
His sharp fork releasing evil
His fiery face burning his skin
His evil smile smirking at you
His goatish voice repeating where we are
His pointy head being stroked
His house being burnt by fire
His clickety hooves stepping towards you
His slithery tail slapping the floor
His monobrow looking at you.

Joe Murphy (11)
Herne Bay High School

Christmas Is Near

Christmas is near
It's nearly here
It's soon arriving
It's getting more exciting
I hope I get a cat or dog
Or even a toad or frog.

I can't wait anymore
It's really a bore
Shall I write a note to Santa Claus
But will this note reach his door?
Just two more days
I'm waiting to say,

Mum, Dad, it's *Christmas Day!*

I wake up in the morning,
Look out the window, what do I see
It's all white and snowy,
Mum, Dad, what day is it today?
Well, little one, it's
                              Christmas Day!

Megan Rose Grosvenor (11)
Herne Bay High School

Lobsters

Lobsters should have something to say,
Before we decide to call it a day,
We can't just throw them in a pan,
Because their lives are clean and clear,
Their googly eyes and their creepy claws,
I adore them, even more,
When we let them live their lives outdoor,
So stop killing *lobsters!*

Fikriye Karagozlu (11)
Herne Bay High School

I Am

I am Ben
I wonder, how did God make us?
I hear my mum's voice
I see everything God made
I want an electric scooter
I am Ben
I pretend to be a bird
I feel bad
I touch the Statue of Liberty
I worry about getting into trouble
I cry when I am lost
I am Ben
I know I like English
I say OK
I dreamt that I had an electric scooter
I try to go out straight after school
I hope I get home
I am Ben.

Ben Haddon (11)
Herne Bay High School

The Tramps In The Street

They beg for change in your pocket,
They live in narrow alleys in boxes,
They dig in your litter bin, next to you
Like hungry little foxes.

Sometimes they play guitars
And sing with a crippled voice
And see with their scornful eye
A man in a Rolls Royce.

Some tramps can afford some food
Some tramps can be little crooks
Some tramps are jolly and happy
So the world isn't as bad as it looks.

Matthew Nayler (11)
Herne Bay High School

The Winter

Winter is often horrible, rainy and cold,
Nothing to do outside the house,
We can't go out to play at school,
Play football or go on the climbing wall,
It's so miserable you can't see your friends,
Until all of the winter ends.

Sometimes it's not quite so bad,
When the snow falls and you can play
Throwing snowballs in the sun,
Snowflakes falling for everyone,
All together snow is lots of fun,
Together we can play and run.

Also winter can be fun indoors,
Drawing pictures and playing games
Watching television at night,
Lots of friends you can invite,
To turn your day into a success,
You can write a story to the press.

Really winter can be fun or boring,
There are two ways of looking at it,
If you try you will have some fun,
For all the family and everyone,
Winter can be anything you like,
Just have fun and sing on the mic.

Gareth Rowland (11)
Herne Bay High School

Porsche V Lotus

P orsche v Lotus
O ur cars are really fast
R acing around the track
S kidding all over the place
C oming closer together
H e is winning and I am right behind him
E ngines roaring as we go

V ery hard to see who is going to win this close race

L ook out, here I come
O vertaking fast as I go
T earing round the corner
U sing all the track
S traight ahead and I am the winner.

Nathan Dew (11)
Herne Bay High School

My Horse

Horses are so powerful,
On and on go their feet.
Riding them gives me a treat,
Soft tail, soft mane,
Eager to go riding in the rain,
So powerful, so strong, I love them!

All of them are so strong
Riding them, clip-clopping feet
Everybody loves horses!

Nicolle Quinlan (11)
Herne Bay High School

Hallowe'en

Hallowe'en,
All Hallows Eve.
They're all the same,
petty is each name,
trying to cover,
the horror of that fearsome night,
where footsteps follow you,
never ceasing.
Ancient graves empty,
their owners as silent as mice,
creeping around parks, preying on lonesome children,
as their victims.
Hallowe'en,
All Hallows Eve,
they're all the same,
petty is each name.

Charlotte Burch (12)
Herne Bay High School

Football

The atmosphere starts
The ball rolls
The players chase
The wild fans
The strict ref
The glimmering trophy
The ball floats
The final kicks
The dramatic finish
The whistle blows!

Joe Nelder (11)
Herne Bay High School

I'm Fast

I'm fast, I am furious
I'm luxurious
I'm brave and true
I might like you
I'm Sam
I'm the man
I'm from the east side
Not the west side
I am the best!
From the east and the west
I told you
I'm a soldier
If you like that, put your hand in the air
If you don't get the hell out of here
I'm like a cheetah
I'll beat you
Peace!

Sam Stickings (12)
Herne Bay High School

Horses!

Cosy stables, full of hay,
Noisy feeding, all teeth chewing,
Fields and fencing, so lush and hard,
Thick manes and tails, long and tangly,
Clean grooming kits, full of all the brushes,
The silky fur that's been tampered with,
Leathery saddles and bridles, so heavy most of the time,
My hard helmet, protecting my head,
Rubbery sandy riding school, helping my horse to learn,
The showing and the gymkhanas . . . I've got
                          butterflies in my stomach!

Emily Meyer (11)
Herne Bay High School

That's My Mother Standing There

(This poem is dedicated to Lynn Potter)

That's my mother standing there,
With her shiny, dark black hair,
Swaying like a chain of leaves,
In the gentle summer breeze.

That's my mother standing there,
With her warm, hazelnut eyes,
Shimmering like a crystal,
Under a ray of sunlight.

That's my mother standing there,
With her soothing voice,
Calming like the sound of waves,
Washing all of your problems away.

That's my mother standing there
And I am next to her,
When I grow up I want to be,
. Exactly like my mother.

Megan Potter (12)
Herne Bay High School

Football

Red and shining kits.
Old Trafford at its best.
Crowds, getting more bloodthirsty.
Players, getting more hot.
Fast food is going around.
The goals are now found.
Blind ref is annoying the crowd.
Battered ball lies on the ground.
The final shot.
Manchester United are going to win.
Then the shot . . .
           They scored!

Shaun Westwood (11)
Herne Bay High School

Star Signs

The glistening scales of Pisces
The pointed horns of Taurus
The metal bowls of Libra
The strength of Aquarius
The soft fur of Leo
The beauty of Virgo
The silent bleating of Capricorn
The creepy crawl of Scorpio
The confusion of Gemini
The archery talent of Sagittarius
The side walk of Cancer
The hard head of Aries
The sparkling stars in the night sky.

Kira Mandon-Gassman (11)
Herne Bay High School

Football

The ferocious roaring crowd.
The angry manager.
Grass so soft and silky.
Goals waiting for the ball to come.
Tasty food at its best.
The red, shining kit.
Blind referee annoying the crowd.
The golden ball, battered and worn out.
Talented players always scoring.
The glittering stadium.
They've shot, they've . . .
missed!

Paul Harris (11)
Herne Bay High School

I Am

I am very annoying because I never do my homework
I wonder if I will get to see my friends from my old school?

I hear my old cat
I see a lorry
I want to drive a lorry
I am very annoying because I never do my homework

I pretend to drive in the car
I feel my cat's paw
I touch a bar of chocolate
I worry if I will get to see my friends from my old school
I cry because my cat has died
I am very annoying because I never do my homework

I know that my friends will keep in contact with me
I say that I will drive a lorry
I dream about going to America and drive a race lorry
I try and make my handwriting
I hope that people in Africa will get food and drink
I am very annoying because I never do my homework.

Ricky Wood (11)
Herne Bay High School

Ghosts

The dead victims
Their bloody deaths
Their screeching cries
Their fallen-off heads
Their killing hands
Their haunted minds
Their horrid laughs
Their excellent finds
Their silent walk
Their spooky house.

Ceris Cook (11)
Herne Bay High School

First Day Of School

On my first day of school
My nerves were nervous
I was shivering and shaking
Like I was in the Arctic Ocean
I was locked behind icy-red bars
No escape
An eternity at school
For I was . . .
Trapped!

The day lasted forever and ever
Ring, ring, ring the bell went,
Time to go home
Whoops, it was just registration.

Ashley Jordan (11)
Herne Bay High School

Cats

Their fluffy, puffy fur,
Their glistening diamond eyes,
Their squashy button nose,
Their sharp, pointed teeth,
Their silly, stupid smile,
Their long, twitching whiskers,
Their annoying, mumbling noises,
Their beautiful, soft paws,
Their crooked, clumsy walk,
Their swishy, swerving tail,
Their soft noise of purring.

Cloé Ashtari (11)
Herne Bay High School

My First Day At School

I went to school one day,
There were lots of big kids in my way.

Then it turned break time,
We all ran out in a hurry.

We then had history, not science and not art,
Then the bell rang and then we did depart.

Lunchtime has now arrived to go and eat outside
I ran outside and didn't go to lunch. I cried!

I started to run towards my maths class,
And when I got there I wanted to know whether I'd passed.

Then I went to my last lesson, French
I got a merit, I was impressed.

I finally got home and sat down to rest.

Laura Clark (11)
Herne Bay High School

War!

The outstanding deaths
The roaring noises
The ferocious artillery
The unbearable suffering
The shimmering guns
The heavy footsteps
The life they left behind
The propaganda they told
The diplomatic feuds
The unbreakable alliances
The useless peace treaty they signed!

Darrell A Hogbin (12)
Herne Bay High School

First Day Of School

It was the first day of school
It was the worst of all
I was in a mess,
People said, 'Oh bless.'

It was the first lesson
It was technology
Then boring biology
Then the bell rang.

Children ran
There was a *bang*
I was on the floor
But people begged for me
As I cried for help.

I wish I could be tall
Instead of being small
I got hit by a ball
I was a fool.

I got hit on the head
I felt tired
And wanted to go to bed.

Avinish Sheo-Rattan (11)
Herne Bay High School

Football

Sitting in the seats of Old Trafford
A drink in my hand.
The roaring of the crowd filling the stadium
A decisive referee waiting to start the match
A rush of wind blowing past my face.
The whistle blows.
Some professional players start chasing the ball.
The match has begun . . .

Luke Holland-Batt (11)
Herne Bay High School

The Forensic Scientists

There's been a murder
That the police can't solve.
They call on the forensics
Who are down right away.

They go to the crime scene.
They leave no stone unturned.
Then they gather the clues.
Fingerprints, weapons, whatever they find.

There's been a murder
That the police can't solve.
They call on the forensics
Who are down right away.

They go back to the lab.
Analyse the DNA.
Examine the prints.
They have their suspect.

There's been a murder
That the police can't solve.
They call on the forensics
Who are down right away.

They call on their suspect.
They show him their warrant.
They search the house.
They've found the weapon.

There's been a murder
That the police can't solve.
They call on the forensics
Who are down right away.

They take him to court.
They tell the judge their clues.
The jury decides where he goes.
He goes to prison, caught by the scientists.

There's been a murder
That the police can't solve.
They call on the forensics
Who are down right away.

Miles Smith (11)
Herne Bay High School

Cat

The speed, the power,
She can change from gentle to rough
Her curly tail
Her soft coat
Her moonlit eye
Shining so bright
Her sharp but lethal claws
Her independent mind
The cat.
A mysterious creature!

Jadie Browning (12)
Herne Bay High School

Dragonball Z

The good defending
The evil attacking
The powerful energy
The people crying
The earth shaking
The super speed
The energy blasting
The powers roaring
The fight's over
The good have won!

Lloyd Waldron (12)
Herne Bay High School

Art

Forget all my problems,
In the distance, from the radio I hear a song,
I decided a long time ago,
That here among the paints and colours is where I belong.

Relax my mind,
Comfortable in my seat,
Pick up a paintbrush,
Keep it neat.

Some people don't like me,
Some think I'm smart,
And some people like me,
But I don't care, I just like art.

Anita Suzanne Tuffen (12)
Herne Bay High School

The Silent Horse

The golden hay
The grazing foals
The feet pace
The kicking doors
The rich fields
The wet feed
The shiny bridle
The leather saddles
The fabric rug
The silence of the horse
The wind blowing in your face.

Vicki Ford (12)
Herne Bay High School

My First Day At School

My first day at school was really great,
It was a good job I was not late,
The teachers are all very smart,
They let us all join in and take part.

English, maths and ICT
And also including geography,
Were really great and enjoyable
Not like most lessons at school.

Coming to the end of the day,
Tomorrow the next time we have play,
Children rushing out the door,
But mopping the floor is the janitor.

Kloe Williams (11)
Herne Bay High School

Trick Or Treat?

H ave a trick or a treat, water bombs or candy bars.
A t midnight you can hear an owl and
    maybe the screaming of the ghosts around.
L ight up the pumpkins, get ready for a fight.
L ots of scary costumes and the full moon.
O ld gravestones and rotten bones.
W itches, goblins and scary ghosts.
E ven the toughest of people get scared
    when they hear the noises of Hallowe'en night.
E nveloping mist down the street.
N early done, the sun is coming up
    Hallowe'en is sleeping for one more year.

Marie Diamond (12)
Herne Bay High School

First Day Of School

My first day of school was frightening
It hit me like thunder and lightning.
I met three of my mates
And we talked about our fates.
The bell rang and we were led to the hall,
I had a headache, I wanted to fall.
One by one we were called in to our tutors,
After all the talking we all wanted muters.
We went to lessons three and four
I really wanted no more!
At lunch we bought a bunch of things.

It was over now
I just thought *wow*
I got on the bus
Without a fuss
It was all done
Not really was it over
We had a full year ahead
Arghhhhhhhhhh.

Dexter Muller (11)
Herne Bay High School

What Is Death?

Why does it haunt me so?
Why do people I love have to go?
What happens after death?
Where do we go?
Is it pain?
Is it pleasure?
Is it good or bad?
So why, oh why, do the people I love have to go?

Lara Warne (12)
Herne Bay High School

Abuse

I sit alone in my room,
On my bed,
With the clock's hands growing fainter,
Fainter,
Fainter,
His hands stop ticking,
His face watches me,
Tears build up behind my bloodshot eyes,
3, 2 . . . 1,
I explode!
Tears flood my room,
Loud sobs echo around the house,
I look up at the ceiling,
And long to be hanging from it.
Pictures of my friends fill my head
And yet again I am full of dread
Of what would happen
If I were to die!
My friends would cry and sob,
Like I am now.
My mother and father will be back soon,
I had better clean quickly,
And hide from the terror . . .
My parents!

Michaela Corcoran (12)
Herne Bay High School

Sports Cars

The respectable AC Cobra,
The roar of a V8 Shelby Mustang GT-500,
The sensational Morgan Aero 8,
The legendary Mercedes-Benz CLK-GTR,
The wicked McLaren F1,
The memorable Corvette Sting Ray,
The streamlined Ferrari Enzo,
The drivers are tense,
The crowd is wild,
The smell of burnt rubber,
The cars line up,
The flag goes down,
The race begins.

Laurence Decker (11)
Herne Bay High School

Football

The burning crowd,
The aggressive players,
The glittering lights,
The roaring stadium,
The fast referee,
The speedy striker,
The suffering manager,
The round football,
The glistening white goal net,
What a goal!

Sophie Wellings (12)
Herne Bay High School

Thank You

(Dedicated to Katrina Reynolds)

I'm not the kind of person
Who can easily say
What their feelings are
So I will try to write down
What I want to say
We have been through ups and downs
Usually more ups than downs
But through it all you have been there
I've been upset and stressed
I've been violent and ill
Yet you have never given up on me
You have listened to me
You've given me help whenever you could
You've given me advice
You have put up with my tantrums
You have always looked after me
It can't have been easy for you
You always make sure
That no matter what
I will always end up laughing
I just wanted to say
That I couldn't have survived without you
Thank you.

Kathrine White (16)
Herne Bay High School

The Man From Eden

There was a man from Eden
Who sat down on his reading
He took a big blow
And stopped the flow
That was the man from Eden!

James Barrett (12)
Herne Bay High School

I Was Trapped

The burning flames,
The fierce heat,
The kitchen alight,
Frightening atmosphere,
I was petrified,
Faint noises,
It was gloomy and dark,
Flames surrounding me,
I heard the fire engine pull up,
He smashed through the door,
He grabbed me and took me out,
The crowd roared!

Chelsea Wibberley (12)
Herne Bay High School

Food

Roast dinner smothered in gravy,
Spaghetti Bolognese with Ragu sauce,
Floppy, salty McDonald's chips,
Pancakes with sugar and lemon or lashings of golden syrup,
The scrumdiddlyumpscious pizza and hot dogs at a party,
Ice cream for dessert with gallons of chocolate sauce,
Chocolate fudge cake for afters with dollops of cream,
There is the sauce
And there is the spoon,
Let the feast begin!

Harvey Gasson (11)
Herne Bay High School

The Song Of The Ghosts

The hellish skeletons tortured by death -
Body parts splattering everywhere, trying to gain his breath -
Now the end, as the spirits rise -
Looking around as they try to analyse -
Trying to figure out this whole new world -
Hearing the voices shouting aloud -
You are in Hell, you have done wrong -
It almost sounds like voices singing a horror song.

Amy Tickner (12)
Herne Bay High School

Pain Poem

Down in a pain-riddled torture chamber
Rusty, sharp instruments hang from long nails dripping with blood.
Half a corpse lying boneless on a rusty, metal worktop.
Held down with light manacles, jars full of human organs
And a skull stuck in a boiling pot of death.
There were thousands, no millions of lost souls
Brought by Mephistopheles
Pushing the skull into the grasp of the Devil himself.

Thomas Hoople (12)
Herne Bay High School

The Race

The long race
The shouting crowd
My face was dripping with sweat
My stamping trainers
The stiff track
The tired runners
The brilliant finish
The shining, golden cup.

April Vincent (12)
Herne Bay High School

Strange Happenings

Something woke me from my sleep,
Did I really hear it creak?
As I rose from my bed,
I had a glimpse of the dead.

As I sat perplexed and still,
Like I was on some sort of pill
I shut my eyes,
Hoping the thought would vaporise.

I sat out of bed
And said,
'Should I dare go down the stair,
Or just stand and glare?'

I took a step towards the door,
When I heard a creak on the floor,
I dare not take a step more
Or even peek out of the door.

Staring through the windowpane,
I saw a shape in the rain,
Was it a ghost, was it a ghoul?
I really wish I was at school.

'Please don't hurt me,' I shout,
'If only I could find a way out.'
Then there was a hand on my shoulder,
Which made my body go even colder.

Shaking me,
Rattling me,
A voice then came to my ear,
Then soon I realised I had nothing to fear.

I woke from my dream,
To a face with a gleam,
To find it was my dad
Oh how I was glad!

Conor Rourke (12)
Herne Bay High School

My First Day At School

As I walked through the gate,
I wondered whether I was late
I was so scared
But no one cared.

As I went into my tutor room
I felt like I had met my doom!
But my tutor was very nice
Until I found out he had lice.

When the bell went for home time
On the bus my sister asked if I was fine
When I got to my house
My cat had caught a mouse.

Stuart Smitherman (12)
Herne Bay High School

First Day At School

So big, so scary
Don't send me Mum
I'm so small
They're so tall
What if I get lost
I won't come out alive
The school buzzes like
Bees in a hive
The day is long
So much work
So much to do
I'm not going to make it
Argh, but I do!

Danial Morgan (11)
Herne Bay High School

The Ghoul

The ghoul of Crookhill Hall,
Likes to play football,
Up and down the hall,
Though he is not good at all.

He really can't play pool,
Because he is a fool,
He likes to think he's cool,
The ghoul of Crookhill rules.

The ghoul of Crookhill Hall,
Loves to play the fool,
Frightening everybody,
In the swimming pool.

Grant Eldridge (12)
Herne Bay High School

Time

We just need time alone
To be apart
To let us think
To use our minds and figure ourselves out
We need time to adjust
Time to feel and show our feelings
Time to find one another
And time to be just us.

Katrina Reynolds (16)
Herne Bay High School

First Day At School

First day at school,
I wish I were tall,
All the children,
Big and small.

'Excuse me,' I would say,
They'd shout back, 'Get out of the way.'
I was worried and scared
Frightening thoughts soared round my head.

The work was all right,
That gave me delight,
I had nice mates
As I ran through the gates.

Chris Martin (11)
Herne Bay High School

Ghosts

Ghosts are things that never care,
Even when they give you a scare.
Walking through walls day and night,
Most folks get an awful fright.
Floating, white sheets, *ha* what a laugh,
I never knew that people were so daft.
I don't believe in ghosts, not really,
To me I think it is rather silly.
Although I wonder what I saw that day,
In an empty house, peeking through a doorway.

Robert Campbell (12)
Herne Bay High School

First Day At School

The car door slams shut,
Footsteps I hear they turn into thuds,
I smell fresh food being delivered,
Two gates open, more footsteps . . .
Bang! The gates had shut!

Walking to the big hall
By the door.
Was Mrs Moore
239 children were there,
Since they took me captive
I haven't been very reactive
After a while my lessons are over.

James Smith (11)
Herne Bay High School

My Scary Ghost Poem!

My scary ghost is called Gale Gilow
She wanders at 12 midnight.
You see her standing on the galleried landing,
Waiting to give someone a terrible fright!
The thunder struck and Miss Gilow tripped up,
That's the last you saw of her!
She tries to spook you out when you are alone.
Gale Gilow is a frightening ghost,
She haunts in the deepest, darkest night!
Beware, beware, she floats up there!

Sarah Back (13)
Herne Bay High School

Sports Cars

The noisy, revving engine,
The 6.2l driving down the road,
The horrendously large spoiler,
The massive exhaust,
The jumping and bouncy suspensions,
The car of my dreams,
Tinted up windows,
What incredible speeds,
What's in front of me?
I can't see.
Then the horrific crash happens
Then the horrible death.

Michael Dance (12)
Herne Bay High School

Headless Horseman

The headless horseman rides the streets.
Terrorising all he meets.
In the darkness of the night.
He turns to the left, then to the right.
The horse can navigate the way,
Cause the rider can't see, night or day.
In battle fierce he lost his head,
He's searching for it now he's dead.
When he finds it he can cease,
And settle down in ghostly peace.

Daniel Horton (12)
Herne Bay High School

Be Careful It Could Be The End!

There was an old teacher called Sally-Ann,
That got found under the ground,
She could be haunting you now.
When people get told they always say *wow!*
She opened the basement door
And fell right the way down,
All that was there was all of her bones and bits
All of her arms and legs were like sticks,
This must warn you not to go down in a basement again,
Or you could be looking towards the end!
Beware of ghosts!

Nicole Gardner (12)
Herne Bay High School

Roller Hockey

Squeaky wheels
Thumping sticks
Roaring crowd
Cuts and nicks
Referees wrong
Hockey players right
All over a stupid fight
Whistle blown
The game starts
Passing and shooting
Score goes up.

Myles Tichband (12)
Herne Bay High School

Best Friends

Best friends share their secrets,
Best friends always play,
Best friends send you postcards,
When they go away.

Best friends go round each other's houses
Mostly for tea,
Best friends may comfort each other
When they get stung by a bee.

Best friends look at each other's clothes,
Best friends are always borrowing things,
And best friends may even want to sing.

Best friends go into each other's rooms
And sleep on each other's beds
And one time they may decide to camp
In each other's sheds.

Best friends know what the other is thinking
And know what's on their minds,
They always let each other join in
And never leave them behind.

Best friends wait and they hold the door
All of this tells you, what friends are really for . . .

Chelsea Penn (12)
Rainham School For Girls

Day And Night

In the day the sun comes out to shine,
All the world is out to play.
And in the night the sun goes to sleep
And the dark, evil moon
Comes out and all the world goes to sleep.

Thomas Childs (11)
St Anselm's RC School, Canterbury

A Few Days In The Life Of A Flour Baby

(Inspired by Anne Fine's Flour Babies)

Last week I was created.
I could not see or hear.
My nose was all serrated
And I only had one ear.

I was given to a pupil.
He laughed when he saw me.
He dressed up in hoodlum clothes
And then he laughed with glee.

I looked a real idiot -
A girl dressed like a boy!
'Wait until my friends hear this!'
I said, but without joy.

The very next day I went to school
'Twas not a fun affair -
I ended up getting sat upon
And ruining my hair.

When I got back I learnt that pain
Can come completely free -
I was bitten by a doggie
And was sent to casualty.

I came back with my legs in cast
And a bandage for my toes.
My arm was in a cotton sling
With an attachment for my nose.

And so here ends my tale of woe
I'm glad I'm still alive.
I'm waiting very thankfully here
For my getaway to arrive!

Thomas Dewey (12)
St Anselm's RC School, Canterbury

The Seasons

Summer and Winter argue away
They say, 'I want the whole year to rain,
So that people will be cold and sad.'
'No,' cried Summer, 'I can't let you!'
'I want the year to shine all the time.'
Summer and Winter became angry,
Then Summer decided that they should,
Go to Mount Olympus to Zeus.
Winter told Zeus about their problem.
He thought for a moment and then cried out,
'Summer, you will have six months to shine
And Winter, you shall have six months to rain.'
Winter and Summer agreed with Zeus
And that is why we have the seasons.

Isla Cross (12)
St Anselm's RC School, Canterbury

The Day Night Became!

Once the planet was much too hot,
People just sat and stared,
In Heaven there was no rest at all
For God really cared!
He needed to find a solution
He really needed to think
Of something that could give the people
Time to rest in the cool!

'Yes!' he screamed with glee,
'There can be a time halfway through the day
When the sky will be black
And the sun will hide away
Out will come a moon
And then it will be *night!'*

Sarah Tutt (11)
St Anselm's RC School, Canterbury

Day And Night

Dungeon of brightness
Let the sun go
We're bored of night
Tired of night
Please, please
Please let her go!

Dungeon of brightness
Take her back
We're sweating
Dying because of her
Please, please
Please take her back!

We need the day
We need the night
So let her go
Then take her back.

Rebecca Stiffell (11)
St Anselm's RC School, Canterbury

Diamonds

The sun makes it bright and hot in the day,
Then the moon comes out and the sun goes away.
The clouds are like cotton wool rolling by
And the stars are like diamonds in the sky.

From dusk to dawn, we have moonlight,
From dawn to dusk, we have daylight.
Rockets go to the moon, but not to the sun,
Because if we did, we'd be cooked - very well done!

Stephanie Gawler (11)
St Anselm's RC School, Canterbury

How A Bee Created The Seasons

The snow lies thick on the ground,
Deep silence is all around.
Not one living thing to see,
Except for a lonely bee.
So it invents a flower,
But soon, after one hour,
It dies.

So the bee creates a sun
Bee makes a plant, just for fun.
The leaves spread forming creepers,
So bee creates plant eaters.
Those creatures are getting fat
So bee makes animals that . . .
Eat them!

Animals are all around,
In the sky, deep sea and ground.
But bee has no time to laze,
He carries pollen these days
Poor little bee is worn out
But flowers just mock and shout
Poor bee!

Bee has really had enough!
He kills all the plants in a huff,
Which kills all the animals
Frogs, cats, donkeys and camels,
They are no longer around,
The snow lies thick on the ground.

Peter Matthews (11)
St Anselm's RC School, Canterbury

Daytime

Every day it's just the same old thing,
Wake up, stay around all day, then go back to sleep.
No one ever thanks me, thanks me for keeping them alive,
For helping them to grow crops to feed their children
And to keep them bright and happy.
No one ever thanks me
I go to sleep and my only friend, the moon, rises
We change shifts like two ships passing in the night
But even then I still have my jobs
I sit behind the moon and shine
My light flickers round his body like a leopard chasing prey
And in the morning it all starts again
And I just get sadder and sadder
Yet still nobody thanks me.

Hugh Molloy (12)
St Anselm's RC School, Canterbury

The Gift Of Light

Long ago all the animals got presents in a little box,
Fields stretching far were given to the fox.
The owl got trees as far as you can see
And the gift of wings was given to the bee.
Out of all the presents each animal got one,
But the silly, little elephant was really rather dumb.
He kept it to himself indeedy,
He was being awfully greedy.
Eventually he opened it a bit,
To find some light coming out of it.
The light gave us day but when elephant went to bed,
The wind blew across and the box shut like lead.
So that gave us night, but when elephant wakes,
He opens the box and day it makes.

Zoë Buckland (11)
St Anselm's RC School, Canterbury

Day And Night

A very long time ago, when there was only day,
A very long crocodile couldn't sleep while he lay,
He scratched, he yawned, but he still couldn't sleep,
When an ant came past and said, 'Take a peep!'

It was a large, shiny bag with a blue inside,
It had a purple handle with ribbons.
'What is this?' the crocodile cried.
'It's horrid, it's scary,' the ant replied.
'It's that thing, that only the underworld have, it's called night!'

Then the ant scurried off and dropped the bag,
The crocodile grabbed it and hit it,
He thought and he thought about the bag,
It wouldn't really matter if he had just one peep
She he untied, untwisted, scary bag, *booooooooo!*
The night had fallen out.

It was scary, it was horrid,
It was like Hell at that moment,
The ant was right,
The crocodile screamed and yelled that he wanted day,
When finally it came,
From that day on we have day and night.

Anna-Lisa Stiffell (11)
St Anselm's RC School, Canterbury

The Seasons

Spring is the time when the flowers appear
The sun is hot now that summer's here
The leaves all fall in windy autumn
But it's now freezing cold because it's winter.

Spring is back and animals are here
But it's back with the sun now summer's appeared
Put on jumpers, for again it's autumn time
But now it's present time because of winter.

Kate O'Leary (11)
St Anselm's RC School, Canterbury

The Day Darkness Fell

Now spring is here Persephone is here strolling across the meadow,
Now flowers have come, Persephone has come
And the winter snow is long gone.

Persephone is sitting under the tree with her mother in the shade.
It's hot, children are playing, having fun
Her long, black hair gleaming in the sun,
For summer is here and winter is long gone.

Here comes autumn, Persephone is now leaving for the Underworld
She is dreading it, wishing she hadn't eaten from Pluto,
Master of the Underworld, for now she has accepted his welcome.
The wind blows as hard as it can until, eventually,
The leaves fall and darkness comes.

Persephone is still in the Underworld,
It is winter even though it has brightened down there
For Persephone is there.
Pluto is happy.
Persephone is happy as she has grown to love him
And now she is waiting, waiting, waiting for spring to come.

Natasha Usherwood (11)
St Anselm's RC School, Canterbury

Night And Day

Night is dark because every 24 hours
A massive man, the size of half of the world
Floats through the sky, blocking the sunlight
That's why it is dark at night
And we call it night because
The man would say, 'Night,' at 12 o'clock.
Day is sunny because a woman
Makes a fireball with her magic.

Thomas Solley (11)
St Anselm's RC School, Canterbury

The Seasons

How the seasons come and go,
This, it seems, is how it begins,
A seed is born in spring,
The season of new life,
It is fresh, new and starting to grow.
As it is new it allows its surroundings to start again,
So they can regain freshness and grow together,
New once more, like a baby.

As everything grows a little more,
It is all bright and in full bloom, once again,
Everyone is happy like a little child playing and laughing,
The seed is now a flower
It calls now, the smiling, carefree, summer sun,
Everything and everyone else are too in full bloom,
Enjoying lazy summer days.

As it grows older still,
More worries creep into its life,
The fresh green glade on trees
Turn into brown shrivelled leaves instead.
It becomes like an adult
Fretting over taxes and relationships
The coldness of winter is creeping around the corner.
As it becomes only bare, frail and old,
It is like an old person,
Full of throbbing aches and pains,
Now cold, harsh, thrashing winter is all it has to live for,
Until it dies for a short time
And is reborn in spring,
The season of new life.

Lucy Vallely (11)
St Anselm's RC School, Canterbury

Summer And Winter

When it's cold, the creatures go away and go to the evil Queen Drusilla
when it is summer, the creatures escape from their cages,
smile and go to their homes in the Blossom Palace.
The sky was baby-blue with a large, yellow circle
in the corner of the blue sheet.
Parony the *Lord* of the sky,
whipped a black, glittering curtain across the sky.
Drusilla captured the creatures and took them to her castle
for six months, the creatures were hungry, tired and worn out.
But Drusilla was whipping them with her snake-like fingers.
The rain started to dribble onto the snail's window
and the snail started to cry, 'Come back little ray of sun, we need you.'
The snail cried all of those six months,
then his wishes came true.
Parony, the *Lord* of the sky whipped another curtain of baby-blue
on top of the black.
All the creatures went back to their Blossom Palace
and had a cup of tea.
So in the winter the little snail cries its wish
and makes it summer again and it repeats this every six months.

Jessica Belfiore (11)
St Anselm's RC School, Canterbury

Little Bo-Peep

A long, long time ago
There lived a girl with a bow,
She was called, Little Bo-Peep
And played all day with her sheep.
Now these sheep weren't ordinary
These sheep weren't dumb
They made plants grow flowers and fruit
But the problem was they never would come.
Now one day Little Bo-Peep
Was very tired and fell asleep
But when she woke her sheep had gone
And it was cold and bitter and there was hardly any sun
So she called to her sheep, 'Come back, you idiots!
The sun's gone away, oh there's no time to play.
I need you here!'
And as she called they all appeared
And plants began to grow and bloom,
And the birds started singing that same old tune.
So she asked her sheep, 'Oh where were you?
Oh where, oh where, oh where?'
And once they'd all turned up at last
They bleated, 'We were at the tree in Africa eating juicy pears!'

So that's how summer and winter come and go
And that's the story of the sheep of Little Bo's.

Sophie Mitchell (11)
St Anselm's RC School, Canterbury

Seasons

Winter
During the day
One could say
Apollo rises
High above the tides
While down below
Down in the snow
Demeter waits
For Persephone to show.

Spring
As Pluto pleas
On his knees
Begging for her to stay
While she smiles gay
And goes to meet her mother
Who goes through the bother
Of growing things for her.

Summer
In the early night
Apollo sleeps
Yet Demeter and Persephone bright
Bring primroses out
To look as they run about.

Autumn
As warmth dims
Demeter grows grim
As she watches Persephone play
That there is the day
When it starts over again.

Solumtoochi Ebenebe (11)
St Anselm's RC School, Canterbury

Night And Day

The sun blazed down on the fields every day
One day a girl said to the sun,
'Sun, oh sun, I'm sure it would be fun to invite moon round.'
'I'm sure it would,' the sun understood,
The people of the world were quite tired.
The moon came round with a frown,
The sun explained to the frowning moon and then disappeared.
The sun stayed there and did not care
Until the people cried out, 'Sun, you're too hot
Believe it or not, go back to your lands!'
The sun went back home and the moon went too
And the people grew tired when the sun stayed still.
So the sun and the moon swapped now and again
And the people of the world never complained.

Alice Crocker (12)
St Anselm's RC School, Canterbury

My Dad

My dad is as strong as an oak tree,
With eyes like a hawk's,
As fat as a drum
And annoying like a fly.
My dad can dictate like Hitler did,
Be as boring as history,
He's as common as the letter E in the alphabet
And as smelly as an old sock.
My dad is lazy like a sofa,
If he were a car he would be an old banger
And when he gets angry he's like the colour red,
He can be loud and large like an American.
My dad can be as nasty as Scrooge from *A Christmas Carol*
And as sharp as my pencil sharpener in my pencil case,
If he were a type of food he would be horrible like sushi,
But nevertheless he is my dad and I love him!

Daniel Ostridge (11)
Sir Joseph Williamson's Mathematical School

Computers

They are very great,
You could have it up to date,
There are many accessories for a computer,
They are sometimes used by commuters,
Such as compact disks and floppy disks,
Sending e-mails might not be worth taking the risks,
People load up computers quick,
Some things sent to you, just make you sick!

People say some websites are class,
But some just don't pass,
I like computers which have the Internet,
Sometimes it shows you football goals
With the ball in the back of the net,
You may be able to watch a film that isn't on a television set,
On a computer you could place a bet,
Shopping is easy on the Internet
You only need to buy things just by a click of a button,
It is easy they just deliver it to your door
Including your Sunday mutton.

Balwinder Singh Rangi (11)
Sir Joseph Williamson's Mathematical School

My World War

When he gets to Heaven,
Saint Peter he will tell,
'One more soldier reporting Sir,
I've served my time in Hell.'

Death is what the Nazi's bring,
Killing freely without a doubt,
But in the end we beat them
British soldiers true and stout.

Alexander Erdogan (11)
Sir Joseph Williamson's Mathematical School

Raptor

He watches, waiting patiently for his prey,
His small, beady eyes scanning like that of a hawk
Snap!
A twig,
The raptor turns immediately; it's a small dog,
Perfect for his insatiable appetite,
He quickly hides from sight,
The dog, is also looking for a meal and is unaware of the raptor,
The raptor's mouth, dripping with drool, is ready,
Ready for an attack,
He alters his powerful legs in the direction of the dog,
He starts to walk,
Jogs
Runs swiftly for the dog, jaws open,
Its scythe-like claws rip the skin
And kills in an instant,
The once clean sharp, razor-like teeth are buried in flesh,
He eats quickly before the rest of the pack come
And scavenge on his prize!

Rory Parsons (11)
Sir Joseph Williamson's Mathematical School

My Sister

She moves like a swan, graceful and true
My Boudicca
She looks like a flower, but she stings like a bee
My refrigerator
Like a roast dinner, she warms me up when she smiles
My sofa
As sweet as a Belgian chocolate
My sonnet
She is like a highlighter on a page of writing, brightening up my day
My Niagara Falls
But still she is not perfect . . .

Thomas White (11)
Sir Joseph Williamson's Mathematical School

Tears Of The Innocent

Summer fields once loved, now passed,
Those days we were alive,
The sun shone down upon your face,
Your hands, your nose, your eyes.

The leaves have fallen twice since then
And still the sun remains,
But duller, sunken, dimming light
My memory your face portrays.

The wind in some uncertain voice
Your name in silence cries,
The hand that felled your innocence
Now lost, your troubles lie.

My heart it understands your plight,
The walls of prison drive
Our youthful, young naiveté,
Dark clouds of Heaven hide.

But summer fields we'll see again
When your time is satisfied,
Till then my friend, no hope is lost
Just memories on the tide.

Rebecca Wells (16)
Sir Joseph Williamson's Mathematical School

Autumn Haiku

Autumn the cold month;
Trees abandon their beauty
And make seas of leaves.

Joshua Heyes (12)
Sir Joseph Williamson's Mathematical School

Some Imagination

It's coming! It's coming!
It's really, really coming!
Quick! Flee the city!
Because it's really coming!

I never thought this would happen.
I thought it would never come back.
But now you have to realise
It's really, really coming!

But phew! At least I have
Some time to run away.
Just run! Run! Run! I think
Because it's really coming!

I am really running now
I'm going to escape
And maybe it won't notice
But it's coming! It's coming! It's coming!

I'm almost at the end of the road
Out of the horrible thing's land.
I'm free! I'm free! I'm free! I'm free!
Oh no! It's really here!

It's standing right in front of me.
It's going to eat me up!
It's standing right in front of me.
The horrible, horrible . . . ant!

Nicholas Ward (11)
Sir Joseph Williamson's Mathematical School

Teacher Dont Care

Every day at schul, Mi works always wong
but teacher dont care.
I spel every thing wrung, Mi ful spots go where I want,
but teacher dont care
Mi grammer gets every time wrung und moi langages get all mix up,
but teacher dont care
Moi homewrks a mess all time, miss words out,
but teacher dont care
order the words get wrung in always I, Mi, commas goe, anywhere, I
like,
but teacher dont care,
Every one gets on moaning abaut mi wrk,
but teacher dont care, no one care,
so y should I?

Adam Owen (12)
Sir Joseph Williamson's Mathematical School

Bully

Bullies to the right of me,
Bullies to the left of me,
There is no way out.
I can only see one thing:
My life, laid before my eyes,
To be banished from this world
By the people who blindly
Do their damage.
So I close my eyes
And take the plunge
To silence the laughter that tortures me so.

Connor Tobin (15)
Sir Joseph Williamson's Mathematical School

My Cat

My cat is not fat
But she likes the odd rat.
If she gets in the way
My dad boots her away.

She eats lots of chicken
She likes grooming and licking.
My sister thinks she is a princess
My sister will end up getting an illness.

She likes having her picture taken
But not being awaken.
She likes catching insects by jumping
She doesn't like to hear a phone ring.

She likes lying on a chair
She gets rid of some of her hair.
She has made at least one nest
She is a bit of a pest.

She is a cute young cat
She likes a small pat.
Caticus is ever so fluffy
My sister calls her Fluffy.

James Donn (11)
Sir Joseph Williamson's Mathematical School

Stars

Stars,
Stars, hang in the night sky.
Stars, stars glitter
And flicker
In the night sky.
Stars, stars bright and
Light in the night sky. They
Shine as I
Sleep.

James Tindall (11)
Sir Joseph Williamson's Mathematical School

Television Shows

There are many television shows,
Some show people living when it snows,
Some show people living with bears,
Everyone in a series cares.
Not just me or you,
Jimmy too.

Some shows are funny,
Actors get paid a lot of money.
Some shows are funny like Simpsons and KHV,
Some funny shows involve cups of tea.

Television shows are also films,
Vampires drinking the blood of their victims.
Jack The Ripper goes for a kill,
During the night in an old windmill.
Some show Godzilla stamping on a car
And someone starts a fight in a bar.

Some shows include sport,
Sportsmen sue each other in court.
Some channels show football and other games,
Each stars a celebrity with famous names.
In horse racing every horse slows,
There are many television shows.

Neil Tanday (11)
Sir Joseph Williamson's Mathematical School

A Memory

I don't understand you,
I don't really know you,
I don't see you with my eyes,
I see you with my heart,
You're an angel from above,
You're a blessing from God,
You're a warming from,
The sun.

Reece Price (11)
Sir Joseph Williamson's Mathematical School

Night-Time Stars

Hundreds of thousands of stars lay in the sky
Meteors, comets and shooting stars go by
The moon illuminates the sky and stars
Everything near it except for Mars
The sun, the earth, the moon, the stars
Are only parts of our solar system
Millions of miles into space still need to be explored
Maybe we'll discover
Space has a core . . .

Michael Robert Green (11)
Sir Joseph Williamson's Mathematical School

Computers

Computers, super high tech, mega powerful, super qualified,
mega cool, super smart, loads of fun, super fast, all in one box.
Two years later, after its prime, it's out-of-date and past its time.

Computers, super load of junk, super slow, mega rubbish,
super dumb, mega unqualified, super low tech, mega weak in one box.
Things change quickly, if you don't keep up, you'll be left behind.
You'll end up like a dead computer, lifeless, unwanted
and dormant in mind.

Edward Brookes (11)
Sir Joseph Williamson's Mathematical School

Hands

Hands are different shapes and sizes.
Hands have four fingers and a thumb.
Hands are crinkly, wrinkly and bony in old age.
Hands are chunky and pink in the young.
Hands can foretell your future.
Hands can reflect your past.
Hands, hands, we all need hands.

Ryan Ellis (11)
Sir Joseph Williamson's Mathematical School

Celtic Warrior

An orange hedge of bushy beards,
An orange hedge of hair,
We Celtic warriors will destroy you,
And take *your* heads and hair.

Our swords will cut your guts to pieces,
And make great holes through your backs,
For we are Celtic warriors,
And leave more than just a scratch.

An orange hedge of bushy beards,
Aint the key to our power,
So bring it on you stupid sissies,
And don't just stand and glower.

Our brains are more evolved than yours,
An' I know how to prove it,
We are way more cleverer than you,
We don't use woad on bruises.

We can use the herbs of power,
And we can defeat you,
Surrender now and we won't have to,
Humiliate and beat you.

Richard Boyle (11)
Sir Joseph Williamson's Mathematical School

Degus Lives

My silly Degus
Trying to chew through metal
Their teeth turn yellow
They eat nuts like squirrels
And they fight like kangaroos
Their bath is sand
Their favourite food is plants
When they go to sleep
They don't make a peep
And snuggle up together.

Joseph Bennett (11)
Sir Joseph Williamson's Mathematical School

Hunter

As peaceful and as quiet as a mouse he lies,
Rigid in the shade of a tree.
His body so rough and his tail so smooth,
The mane so furry and fragile lays still in the wind,
The head watches and waits,
He is waiting,
Still,
With no movement,
He is a stone.
At last,
A rustle,
Movement,
He lifts his head,
Then his front legs followed by the back,
Now his whole body is agile,
Stealthily,
Fast,
But not too.
He starts at a walk,
Then a jog,
Run,
A leap,
The tips of his teeth are hidden beneath the antelope's neck,
He has his lunch,
Then,
As peaceful as a mouse he lies,
He is waiting,
He is a stone.

Axl Pendleton (11)
Sir Joseph Williamson's Mathematical School

Grandma

The skies were blue that September morn
I felt like I had just been born
The happiness within my heart
Even though we had been apart

My memories of how it used to be
When I would sit upon her knee
She would tell me tales of long ago
Of how her childhood had been full of woe

She would wipe my face when full of tears
Share my laughter and my fears
The games we played were rather fun
She would chase me and how I could run

So when I knew she was coming to stay
I knew once more that we could play
My plans, my dreams, I could now share
Because once more we would be the dynamic pair

The day went slowly like a snail
Had my grandma taken the right trail
Her memory was not as good as it used to be
How was I to know if she would ever find me

To bring my grandma back to me
Was all I wanted and it just had to be
But as darkness began to fall
I thought I had no hope at all

Then suddenly as my tears fell
My grandma appeared fit and well
So I was happy as I could be
My lovely Grandma is back with me.

Liam O'Brien
Sir Joseph Williamson's Mathematical School

Somewhere (In Time)

I liked it when we saw the hills
And took the flowers in our hands
And never swam, so never drowned
And nothing that we did was planned.
It was all for love, it was all for one,
You were such a girl back then I drew
From it my thoughts and yours
And held them in my hand until,
I blew a kiss and it got lost somewhere between the moors and me.

It doesn't do much good to cry.
I suppose it could be in the sea,
I'll go looking for it one night
I'll get my torch and take my light
And intake all this cooling air, then smoke one more.
And smell your skin and smell your hair,
Until I lose you through the frost.
I'll do what's best for her; I'll walk until my paths get crossed.

And then your eyes will stare at me,
With sheer finesse and . .
'My God you're beautiful,
You remind me of somebody I used to know,
Hold on a sec, my memory's slow.
She lived down here for a while,
Lord, it's probably twenty years ago now,
Though what I do remember is her smile,
That slightly goofy, cheeky curve,
My tattered clothes and messy hair,
Why? What were you doing with me there?'

God, listen to me rambling on,
Let us head back, it shan't take too long.

Wyndham North (16)
Sir Joseph Williamson's Mathematical School

This Is Not The End

Lying here I realise now,
To life there is a meaning,
But as I leave, I do with peace,
Not being dragged, nor screaming.

As now I hope, it is not the end,
But is a new beginning
And now I know, there is no gift,
Greater than the gift of living.

I'll leave quite soon, as I sleep,
My dearest friends and family,
It is against my wishes that you weep,
For, my life, I have led quite happily.

I have fought in battle, won in war,
I have; loved, smiled, laughed and yelled
About letting my spirit soar
And about this and more I have dwelt.

Dear daughter, how I'll miss you so,
My son, you have made me proud,
The end is near I have to go,
The silence seems so loud.

The meaning of life, I believe,
Is to excel in everything,
In love and friendship, do not leave
All the flying to your wings.

I love you all, I hate to leave,
But it is not the end to die,
Wherever I go, I do believe,
I'll see you there, goodbye.

Jak Miller (15)
Sir Joseph Williamson's Mathematical School

Mighty Warrior

M ighty warrior,
I see you,
G ruesomely killing,
H aughty you cannot be,
T hough you are the best,
Y ou are not proud.

W ith your incredible strength,
A xe in hand,
R ed bloodstained shield,
R earing to kill,
I nvincible thoughts,
O ver your foes,
R ush you forward.

Amit Kanekal (11)
Sir Joseph Williamson's Mathematical School

Monty The Dog

Monty, short for Montgomery,
Is a scruffy dog,
Not a neat and tidy dog.
He's a smelly dog,
Not a perfumed, sissy dog.
He's a mad manic dog,
Not the shy and retiring sort.
He's a friendly, soppy dog,
Not a 'bite your hand off dog'.
He's a loud dog,
Not a quiet, timid dog.
He's a mad and manic dog,
Not the shy retiring sort.
Monty's my dog.

Wiliam Hardie (11)
Sir Joseph Williamson's Mathematical School

My Budgie

He scuttles along
And talks to the wall
Bashing his mirror
Just like it's a ball.

He eats from a bowl
Upon the hour
His favourite event
Is having a shower.

He tweets and he chatters
When we are around
He feels a depression
When there is no sound.

He's yellow and green
And stands on a twig
But with minuscule bones
He's not at all big.

Budgie jumps
And he climbs
Around the room
He flees from flies.

Oh budgie dear
We love you so
You make us smile
You make me glow.

Thomas George (12)
Sir Joseph Williamson's Mathematical School

Fairy Tale

Will, he was a noble chap
Adored by all he knew,
Tall and handsome, kind and fair
With piercing eyes so blue.

One day his father came to him
And told him to decide,
'My son, you've just turned twenty-one
It's time to chose your bride.'

So off he set upon his quest
To find his lady fair,
This would not be a simple task
Of that he was aware.

He searched the towns, he searched the moors
But still he searched in vain,
He could not find his future wife
'Twas driving him insane.

But then one day his luck did turn
He almost gave up hope,
A vision of beauty met his eyes
His heart could hardly cope.

'My dearest maid,' the prince proclaimed
'This ring, I ask, you wear,
And we will make, you can't deny
A pretty pigeon pair.'

Wed were they on New Year's day
The weather served them fine,
Confetti drifted, people cheered
And danced 'til half past nine.

The groom and bride (both full of pride)
Stepped onto the horse and carriage,
Off into the sunset they did ride
To consummate their marriage!

Amy Barker (17)
Sir Joseph Williamson's Mathematical School

Sam Spiteful

There was once a boy named Sam Spiteful,
Who thought rude words were rather delightful,
But once, one day as you'll find out,
He was no longer able to shout.

He was prowling the neighbourhood, as he does,
When he came upon his good old Cous',
But when Sam shouted something rude,
It put Cous' into an outrageous mood.

Up Cous' crept in the midst of the night,
This would be difficult without a light,
Snip-a-dee-snip, snip-a-dee-snip,
It was off with his tongue and his lower lip!

When Sam awoke in the light of the day,
To say a swear word as he lay,
He found he couldn't speak anymore
And so he screamed and ran for the door.

When he found it was good old Cous'.
His anger arose with such a buzz.
Boy, he gave him such a punch,
Serves him right, he thought at lunch.

Richard Stockwell (11)
Sir Joseph Williamson's Mathematical School

In The Graveyard

His muddy boots stamp the leafy ground as he walks.
Heart lost to wonder and sorrow, the stone pillars that represent
The old and forgotten surround him.
And he tries to guess when he will join them.
Soon, he knows.
Bells ring from the spectacular tower beside him.
Yet he knows no joy.
It was taken from him by time
For he never knew the mysterious maiden somewhere beneath his
Feet.
As a cold wind hits his face, he saw his destination across the dirt.
He reaches his place.
Here she lies. Here he places his rose.
'Greetings, my sweet.'
A tear forms in his eye and he struggles to leave but as he does so
He whispers:
'Sleep tight.'
So, the long journey back begins with a clear path ahead,
He is determined to make the journey without turning back;
But he stumbles. His boot's grip failing,
Though his last thought is a happy one:
I'll be with you soon, my love
And he swirls out of thought and time.

John Sharpe (12)
Sir Joseph Williamson's Mathematical School

My Ballad

Sheep now falling into a never-ending sleep,
On board the express is a nightmare.
Not one has the energy to take a leap
Or a mother to feed her baby.

They fall afraid of growing death,
Ununited they stand.
Just like the story of Macbeth,
One will carry until the end.

Now looking towards starvation,
The sheep are getting skinny.
Without the correct co-operation,
Then death is looking certain.

Without the joy of a new home,
And the warmth of a barn,
They look at death in a dome,
In a crowd of many others.

Sheep dying daily, look as if they're crazy,
When they start butting the wall.
Though the sheep may be lazy,
They are able to attack on the ball.

Rejected by many countries,
The sheep lie patiently as if waiting to die.
In the blazing sun,
The creatures will all fry.

With the horror of the end of lives,
They lie down with a nightmare.
A horror of ghosts in a row of five,
Telling the predictions of a happening.

Jonathon Jay (12)
The Duke of York's Royal Military School

Hurricane Isabel

As Hurricane Isabel unleashes all her fury,
All her power,
On the unsuspecting Americans
In less than an hour.

As she hurtles towards Virginia,
Twisting and turning
Speeding through North Carolina,
While she's spinning and churning.

She's the worst of the worst,
Category five,
People fleeing the dreadful storm,
Praying that they stay alive.

Travelling at 115 mph,
Getting closer to the border,
People preparing for her,
Boarding up windows in no particular order.

Six states are waiting,
They're prepared,
Only an hour or two left,
Everyone's scared.

Now she's past America,
Everyone's glad,
Isabel is no more to them,
Everyone's sad.

Now she moves on to Canada,
Further away,
Where is her path?
Where will she stay?

Soon she'll stop,
Stop destructing,
People are rebuilding
Fixing and constructing.

Simon Perrett (13)
The Duke of York's Royal Military School

Gassed!

A phone call at midnight,
Samantha Tolley awoke,
Confused and feeling sleepy,
As her ex-husband spoke.

'Can you hear the mower?'
'Yes,' Samantha replied,
'Can you hear the children?'
They screamed, 'Mummy' as they cried.

As Young hung up,
Sam dialled 999,
This definitely wasn't a case,
To hold her on the line!

Then he rang again,
Policemen standing by,
Samantha suddenly felt sick,
Tears ran from her eye.

'I'll have an abortion,' she cried,
'Things will be OK!'
'It's too late,' he said,
'Dan's dead anyway!'

'Let me speak to my eldest son,'
Sam shouted down the phone.
'I love you, Mummy,' he said,
'And I want to come home!'

One by one they died,
All four children gassed,
At least into Heaven,
Were their innocent souls passed.

Did he have the right
To do this to his ex-wife
Just because Sam wanted
A new and different life?

Hannah Shaw (13)
The Duke of York's Royal Military School

A Soldier's Head

In it there is a battlefield,
With men
Shooting at each other.

And there is
His enemy,
Who shall die first?

And there is,
His entire family,
His entire enemy,
An entire *war!*

There is victory
Or defeat.

There is life,

There is death,

And battles to be fought.

I believe
That a war is not won or lost,
Because each
Side has many losses,
So it is a mighty shame
That so many lives are wasted!

Jason Wild (11)
The Duke of York's Royal Military School

What Am I?

I am like a pancake because I am flat and round.
I am like a Polo because I have a hole through the middle of me.
I am like a mirror because I am shiny.
I am like an encyclopaedia because I store lots of information.
I am like a glass bottle because I am fragile.

What am I?

Richard Garner (11)
The Duke of York's Royal Military School

Top Of A Volcano

It stands there.
A shadowy figure in the night sky,
Tall, dark, full of sadness,
A cooking pot of liquid death.

In the winter, no snow touches it,
Around it a white wilderness lies,
But it remains as dry as bone.
Occasional sparks rise and fall.
It waits and watches.

A distant murmur,
It rumbles and tumbles.
It spews its liquid in a rain of death,
Houses, homes, engulfed in the fiery frenzy.

Slowly it subsides,
Hitting the water with a giant *hisssssssss*
A new layer of rock formed,
Rejuvenating till its next attack.

Iain Whitmell (13)
The Duke of York's Royal Military School

Love

Love is a fire of warmth inside me,
Love glows with the heat of the sun.
With love, you cherish and care for one another,
Relationships build and grow with love.

Love is what keeps us alive and well,
Without love in the world there would be nothing but hate.
Love is passion between two people,
Love is what brings life to this world.

Love is the feeling knowing someone cares for you,
Love is the strongest emotion there is.
Love gives you the power to treasure things dear to you
And love gives you the ability to help others in need of care.

Kelsey Jamieson (11)
The Duke of York's Royal Military School

A Futuristic Office Block

From lush, green grass,
The gleaming glass building soars,
Pointing skywards,
Shadowy clouds,
Chase across the shiny surface

People going in and out of the revolving doors,
The elevator goes up and down, pinging at every stop,
Telephones ringing, kettles boiling to make more tea,
Filing cabinets opening and closing with people waving files,
Bins being emptied and file shredders shredding.

The higher floors look down on the streets,
Cars and people so small,
Computers crashing, hard drives cracking,
Call for the technician, over and over again.

Thomas Bousfield (13)
The Duke of York's Royal Military School

Sports Stadium

Oval arena of conflict, containing hopes and dreams.
The partisan crowds have gathered,
Sounds echo around the tightly-packed stadium.
Red and white carpet is laid and waiting.
The nations' finest elite are ready to take their lanes,
Pressure is building in the pulsating atmosphere.
There is silence.
The starter calls, 'Mark!'
And silence.
'Set!'
Silence.
'Bang!'

James Baber (12)
The Duke of York's Royal Military School

Top Of The Volcano

Standing here, soaring high,
Even above the flattened clouds.
Aeroplanes circling below, about to descend.
The land is so ancient, mud-baked, dry.
Now and then a lizard scuttles across the ashy ground,
Making dust fly.
Bones are scattered here and there,
Birds spiralling in rising streams.
Thin air hurts your lungs.
The steep-edged, volcanic maw
Encloses a death-defying drop,
Only a thin, metal barrier for safety.
Despite the seething, molten mass
The air is so cold!
Freezing ice forms on the extruded rocks.

Joel Sampson (13)
The Duke of York's Royal Military School

Money!

Money is long and round,
Smooth and hard,
Smelly when new,
Lives in piggy banks,
Lives in tills,
Travels far and wide,
Country to country,
Hand to hand.
European, Australian,
I think it's the same.
Different currencies,
Different amounts,
Always makes people scream and shout.
Rare to some, but
Like a click of a finger to others.

Charlotte Sherburn (11)
The Duke of York's Royal Military School

I Feel The Hate Rise Up In Me

Hate is a curse,
The bane of this world.
Hate is a curse,
We need some love.

Pain and despair,
It's in everyone.
Pain and despair,
It's in our soul.

Murder and death,
It's happening now.
Murder and death,
All around me.

Loss and evil,
We can't escape it.
Loss and evil,
It's everywhere.

Tragedies here,
Haven't you noticed?
Tragedies here,
You will see it soon.

James Sykes (12)
The Duke of York's Royal Military School

Bonfire

B onfire crackles and burns
O n the flames they twist and turn,
N othing left, burnt to ash
F right of flames that kill and lash
I n the air, pretty, gleaming, then turns to trash.
R unning children stop and stare
E nding of the flames that fall through the air.

Stephanie Sargent (11)
The Duke of York's Royal Military School

The Moon Is . . .

The moon is . . .

a lump of cheese,
a large golf ball,
a light in a dark hall,
a disciple of Earth,
a giant disk,
a dome of secrets,
a ball of light,
an alien's home,
a field of molehills,
a head of a man,
a toe of a frog,
a top of a pan.

Carl Taylor (11)
The Duke of York's Royal Military School

A Thunderstorm Is . . .

A power cut that goes on then off,
A light but the bulb keeps coming out,
A big puff of smoke that came out of a pipe,
A jug of water that spilt from the sky,
The start of a really bad headache,
Mouldy marshmallows that were thrown into the sky,
A hairdryer where only the cold temperature works,
Ice cubes that fall down from a freezer,
A grey sheet hung over the sky,
Paint that has been spilt and has made splodges of
                        grey and black all over the sky.

Francesca Howie (12)
The Duke of York's Royal Military School

A Thunderstorm Is . . .

Knives and forks yellow with life
Tip-tapping on a window
Clouds arguing
Zeus throwing his thunderbolts
Time to dive under your duvet
Flooding in good thoughts
Parents fighting
Jesus stamping
God at war
Letting our your feelings
Fighting with your best friend
A new chance to start again.

Laura Ann Wakeford (11)
The Duke of York's Royal Military School

The Sun

The sun is . . .
A fireball from a dragon's mouth
A bomb exploded in space
A gigantic egg set on fire
The death of dark
The retreat of the moon
The birth of light
The legion of angels
A flaming ball
The ruler of light
The decider of day.

Susant Gurung (11)
The Duke of York's Royal Military School

Finally The Bell Rings

When will the day end?
For hours I have sat and watched the paint flaking off the walls,
With quick five-minute intervals to look at my watch.

The teacher sits at the front of the classroom,
Writing on the whiteboard,
Listening out for any noise,
Except for the scribbling of pens, as everyone races to finish
their work.

The ticking of the clock gets louder.
The glaring from all over the room begins as everyone tries
to stay awake.
Footsteps can be heard, getting closer as the teacher parades
up and down the classroom,
Waiting to pounce on anyone who may be about to fall asleep.

Suddenly all the pens come to a halt
As everyone begins to prepare themselves for going home.
Finally the bell rings.
Everyone sighs in relief while running out of the door
Without turning back.
Finally we're free for another day!

Abbie McFarlane (13)
The Duke of York's Royal Military School

A Thunderstorm Is . . .

A base drum sounding;
A curtain of cotton wool over the Earth;
A tap left running;
A door being slammed shut;
A waterfall from space;
The condensation on a cold window;
A light flickering on and off;
A black monster reaching out to get you;
A CD reflecting light into the sky;
A deep dark hole.

Naomi Picot-Watson (11)
The Duke of York's Royal Military School

Classroom Behaviour

I shuffle in, I can't be bothered,
To do the work as the teacher hovers,
It's poems again, they're such a bore,
I'd much prefer to paint or draw.

The clock trickles like a tap,
I clench my hands upon my lap,
I watch a fly against the pane,
If I don't get out I'll go insane!

She sets the work, I hear the sighs,
Sat at their desk, everyone tries
To concentrate, although it's hard,
Our teacher stands, keeping her guard.

Snide comments fly across the class,
I sit and stare through the glass,
Planes are thrown towards the front,
She shrugs her shoulders, bears the brunt!

Sam Sinclair (13)
The Duke of York's Royal Military School

Star

So bright the star in the sky,
I wish I could be that high,
It's like a shiny dot in the night,
That is why I get a sight.

The shine on the star is so intense,
That it must be the best,
When it dies it becomes a black hole,
That is why it needs to cool down at the South Pole.
A star can be a man's worst friend
And this is where my poem ends.

Gulshan Rana (11)
The Duke of York's Royal Military School

It

The boy was alone,
Known as 'It' not he,
Sadness gripped his soul,
His light was dim.

No one to love,
No one to care,
Parents long gone,
Works for his poor, pitiful life.

One quiet night,
He decided to go,
Packed his bag,
Disappeared into the dark.

When dawn did break,
A dustbin did shake,
A head appeared,
Covered in tears.

Through the thick snow,
Down a side alley,
Lights everywhere . . . Christmas,
Slowly he walks to the warm church.

A pew to rest,
Lie down and sleep,
Forever.
His light ends . . .

James Ulke (12)
The Duke of York's Royal Military School

Run, Run, Run!

Run to the hills, run for your life,
Bring your kids and bring your wife.
The enemies are coming, take a gun,
Don't waste time, run, run, run!

In the hills, in the caves,
Blood and death is what they crave,
Hear them coming with a battle drum,
Yet again, run, run, run!

In the next town, blood and gore,
They've been here long before,
In the pub, bodies drowned in rum,
Here we go again, run, run, run!

Back to the hills, back to the caves,
Horror and anguish is what they crave
Hear the thudding as they come,
Put on your shoes and run, run, run!

The rival army's taken most of your number,
By now it's night but no time to slumber,
See the fire from a gun,
And this time we won't run, run, run!

Let loose the bullets, shred their lives,
Out of bullets? Pull out your knives . . .
But, now that your life is gone
You are dead, can't run, run, run!

Jamie Kyle Ottaway (12)
The Duke of York's Royal Military School

Another Day At School

From the minute I walk in, I'm sure the clock stops
And as well as the atmosphere, the temperature drops.
The stench of the classroom is hard to bear
With the smell of cigar smoke filling the air.

We get out our workbooks, sit down and stare
At the person we think ugly, with fluffed-up grey hair.
Whatever happens next, is just down to fate,
A limerick, an essay or even a debate?

I look round at my classmates, who are scribbling away
On the front of their prep, which was due yesterday.
No one was bothered about their detention
Because just as usual they were paying no attention.

Five minutes to go, the end's in sight
I might just make it, I can see the light.
Thank God! I'm saved once again by the bell
Now I can get out of this rotting hell!

Claire Riddlestone (13)
The Duke of York's Royal Military School

The Sun Is . . .

A blazing ball of fire
A glowing orange sphere thrown in the sky
A yellow spotlight, glorious and bright
A lemon
A dragon's fiery breath
An orange lamp dangling above the world
Thousands of gleaming orange towels
Rolls and rolls of shining tissue paper
An Oompah Loompahs face staring happily out of the sky
A blonde head turned constantly on the world.

Cerian Halford (11)
The Duke of York's Royal Military School

Autumn

Autumn leaves blowing around,
The cold wind blowing with all its might,
You can hear its sound,
The leaves are blowing with all its height.

The golden brown leaves covering the grass,
The leaves crashing with every blow,
But soon time will pass,
But in the house the fire will glow.

The cold air getting colder as the day goes on,
If you touch the ground you will get a splinter,
The day is short not long,
And soon it will be winter!

Jo Shallcross (11)
The Duke of York's Royal Military School

Seasons

Springtime is near,
Flowers start to appear
And baby lambs are born!

Summer has arrived,
People come alive,
Having picnics on the lawn!

Autumn begins to call,
The leaves start to fall
And here comes the rain!

Winter is slow,
Down falls the snow,
Then it all happens again!

Rachel Wilson (11)
The Duke of York's Royal Military School

Love

Love is a powerful thing
Some claim they know what it means,
How would you describe it?
The person that sits in your dreams?

Love is all about passion,
Of fun and romance combined,
Love is just something that I think everyone will find.

If you said to someone 'I love you,'
Would you love them for eternity?
Love shouldn't only happen
To people gorgeous and pretty.

So the next time someone tells you,
That they'll love you to the end,
Will you just love them back,
Or know that it's 'just pretend'?

Paris Whichelo (12)
The Duke of York's Royal Military School

Volcano

The peak opens,
A gaping mouth,
Exposing the Earth's core.
Molten movement
Of an ancient age,
Ready to explode.
The pinnacle is very fierce.
It will soon erupt,
Engulfing cities,
Melting rock,
Till nature's task is done.

Adam Patrick (14)
The Duke of York's Royal Military School

The Wind Is . . .

The wind is . . .

Swift and smooth,
Fierce as a lion
And as calm as the sea on the calmest day.

The wind is . . .

Week and tamed,
Small as a mouse
And as big as a hippo.

The wind is . . .

Tidy and neat,
Cold as ice
And hotter than lava.

The wind is . . .

Loud and noisy,
More squashed than a hippo in a small box
And as spaced out as air in the world.

The wind is . . .

Wind!

Charlie Joe Parsons (11)
The Duke of York's Royal Military School

The Moon Is . . .

A spotlight in a prison courtyard,
A torch under the duvet covers,
A tilted arch in the distance,
A glaring eye staring mysteriously
A glistening jewel in the night sky,
A light bulb,
A ball of butter,
An island in a black sea,
A bouncing basketball,
A pointed dagger.

Luke Tones (11)
The Duke of York's Royal Military School

The Wind Is . . .

The wind is a winter's day,
    with a cold and blustery spray.
The wind is a rustle of leaves,
    with a gusty breeze.

The wind is clear,
    with a smudgy smear!
The wind is cool,
    with a cloud's faint drool.

The wind is . . .
            cold,
                sharp,
                    and a winter's day!

Sophie Rose Hayes (11)
The Duke of York's Royal Military School

Astronaut's Head

In it there is . . .
'Take off in five minutes.'
A mind like a scrambled egg.
Sickness overwhelming.
Butterflies fluttering.
There is Mars, the big red planet.

There are thoughts of home.
Fear of explosion.
Puzzles of the unknown.

I believe
That only Mars is the one planet we can
Reach.

Thomas Haggart (11)
The Duke of York's Royal Military School

A Typical School Day

It's like a personality changer
Have you ever seen anything stranger?
As soon as you walk through the door
Talking is allowed no more.

'Pens down, books out
There is no need to shout
Now where were we last?
Oh yes, talking about the past.

Please turn to page six in your books,
And don't give me those funny looks.
If you look it's Henry the VIII
Now here is something we can debate.'

I soon drift off into a daydream
Thinking of cakes and ice cream
But soon I snap out of it
Cos this is an important bit.

This drones on for at least an hour
And boy, you use up some brain power!
Then rings the dear bell of enchantment
And the class fills with excitement.

'Right, pack up your stuff
And John, please do up your cuffs.
Get the tables straighter,
Okay, off you go, see you later.'

Holly Watling (13)
The Duke of York's Royal Military School

Raw War

Bombs fall across an ill-fated land,
Families cower there,
Hand-in-hand,
What did we do
To deserve this fate?
Can we stop this
Or are we too late?

Sun shines across a ruined land,
Families wake and wail,
Hand-in-hand,
What did we do
To deserve this fate?
We couldn't stop it,
We were just too late!

Rebecca Garnham (13)
The Duke of York's Royal Military School

A Thunderstorm Is . . .

A rumbly tummy
A running shower
A terrifying monster
A dog's growl
Fireworks with sparks of light
Splinters of water
A dragon's roar
A giant's sneeze
A thunderstorm is . . .
                    wet
                        windy
                            and wild!

Natasha Louise Chapman (11)
The Duke of York's Royal Military School

Since You've Been Gone

Misery and sorrow,
Describe the mood I'm in,
You were lost and found and lost again,
I keep my feelings locked within.

I looked around to talk to you,
But you were not by my side,
Our friendship was untouchable,
In you I could confide.

Staring out the window,
It seems a long way down,
I'd like to jump and end this all,
But I'm afraid to hit the ground.

Since you've been gone, I've lost myself,
It's been downhill all the way,
I've lost my smile and lost my style,
My whole life's gone astray.

I hope you're fine and not too sad,
But now I must decide
How to cope and live with all this grief -
When love and hate collide.

Maybe some other time,
I'll feel a different way,
But here in my delusion,
I can't find the words to say.

Kimberleey Taylor (13)
The Duke of York's Royal Military School

If Stars Were Fish

If stars were fish, they would glisten and pirouette
into the velvet waves of the deepest blue.
They would glide gracefully through the sparkling,
crystal waters and vanish into the lustrous ocean.

If stars were fish, they would dance and sparkle
and fill the deepest darkness ocean with hope and glitter.
Their singing would echo around the world,
then they would congregate one last time
and without a sound they'd be gone into the dismal sounding sea.

Natalie Adams (12)
The Folkestone School For Girls

The Haunting

The mouldy wall leaned forward like the chest of a giant -
black, dirty and scary.
The sea looked so cold, still and green through the old broken window.
You could hear the waves hit each other, they were fast, fierce
and out of control.
Walking slowly, sneakily through the corridor.
Struggling through the thick, tough cobwebs, you would start
trembling, hear the lightning as if it's your own heartbeat.
The light would stun our eyes from the darkness that was in the room.
The floorboards creaked, he jumped to the side of the wall,
it was so damp, bumpy and hard.
He started to feel so scared, it got so cold and windy,
his heart could have blown away.
His mind was all he was using, listening, staring and watching
at every move.
The sound of drops overcame him, he fled towards the door.
Hiding from his own shadow, he ran through the corridor.
He turned around from the sound of scratching bats.
He put his hand on the old, cold and rusty handle,
it dug into his palms.
But he had to be brave, he pulled the door open
and jumped to the other side.

Abbey Langstead (12)
The Thomas Aveling School

56 Croxley Street

I stared into the cracked window, something looked back.
Then I went in, I saw rotting walls, blood dripping from them.
Then I saw a wholesome figure fitting the description of a woman.
I heard the waves crashing against the rocks.
I walked down the basement stairs.
I felt the soft swoop of cobwebs clinging to my face.
I heard a cry, then a thump, I opened the door.
I was horrified, blood dripped from a noose hanging from a beam.
I saw his thin face glare at me as I walked near, his blood-shot eyes
Followed me around the room.
His head was like a rubber ripped in half.
His body was in one corner of the room, his head was in another.

Luke Hooper (12)
The Thomas Aveling School

Dark

The mouldy wall was like a slice of bread
The tall shadow was as dark as a cave
The giant bat was flying as fast as lightning

It was dark
Dark
Dark

The house was as big as an elephant
The doors squeaked like a mouse
The window was letting in light like a big laser beam

It was dark
Dark
Dark!

Ryan Brimsted (12)
The Thomas Aveling School

My Favourite Place . . .

Big towering mountains
Hovering in mid-air,
Leaving the fresh green countryside
In darkness, despair.
Small animals
Lying in the sun and rain,
So quiet, lonely,
So empty and silent,
So dark and so beautiful.

Long, twisting, turning roads
Leading to places maybe unknown.
Houses empty,
Shops and town squares,
Busy or not, it is very entertaining.
Pub drinks,
Singers and dancers,
This is my favourite place.

Jasmine Mason (13)
The Thomas Aveling School

The Haunted House

The dark shadow on the cracked wall
The terrifying bat on the ceiling
I went up the long, broken stairs
A faint figure of a man was standing at the top
I ran back down the long, dark stairs
I ran into the closest room and slammed the door
Thump! Thump!
The man was trying to get in
I looked up at the ceiling
It was a ceiling of eyes, it was all black with little white eyes
The man or thing was still trying to get in.

Carl Rowatt (12)
The Thomas Aveling School

10 Haunt Hill

The creaking from the doors above was creepy
A draught from the slamming doors like a hurricane
Waves were crashing against the rocky cliffs in the distance
Eyes were shining on me like torches
The puddles of blood were as cold as ice
Shadows were jumping from wall to wall in the background
Dust on the floor was as thick as mattresses
White sheets covered the furniture
Sheets that were as white as ghosts
I was scared!

Sophie Funnell (12)
The Thomas Aveling School

Untitled

I opened the dark, creaky door
Then all the pigeons flew away scared.
I could smell blood and heard the blood dripping off the ceiling.
Every step I took a part of the stairs broke off
And I could hear two cats fighting like a war.
I saw a shadow moving under a board.
I went into the room and a dead person was lying on the floor,
Then I thought to myself, *who is moving?*
When I looked on the floor there was a giant hole . . .

Mathew Nicholls (12)
The Thomas Aveling School

The Beach

Soft golden sand slipping through my fingers
Sapphire sea shining like glass
Water filled rocks crawling with crabs
Golden sun shimmering onto thousands of tanned bodies
Ice creams of every flavour and colour
Tropical fish swimming in a pool of glitter.

Katie Arnold (13)
The Thomas Aveling School

The Seashore

Bright blue sky above the stretched out sea
The sun blazing down on the fallen down rocks
Long green grass swaying in the breeze
White-golden sand spread across the beach
Rocks that surround the cliffs
Seaweed lying on the sandy shore
Hilltops covered in sand and grass
The chalk cliffs high above the people
Deep blue sea slapping against the seashore.

Nikki Charlton (13)
The Thomas Aveling School

Paradise Island

The sun made red skies as it disappeared into the darkness
behind the moon.
Dingy little rowing boats lay adrift on the sea.
Small, red crabs scuttled across the sand.
The tall palm trees overshadowed the people below.
The shining sea was clear and beautiful, warmed by the blazing sun.
The tropical fish swam the sapphire waters.
And the golden sand was warm, embedded with footprints.
I heard cries of sadness as we left Paradise Island.

Ashley Jordan (13)
The Thomas Aveling School

A Beach Life

Soaring birds as high as the big fluffy clouds,
The beach glistened in the bright sun,
As the shiny, clean, sparkling car drove past
Reflecting in the sea's blue greatness,
The sound of young, chattering people,
The rough sea slapping the seashore,
The boats moving swiftly on the light blue sea.

Andreas Eliades (13)
The Thomas Aveling School

The Haunted House

The creaking of the doors was like the movement
and sound of a ghost
Doors moved as the shadows came closer
the whispering got louder as the bodies of the people got closer
the creaking was as loud as a screaming baby
on the end of a firework.
Dampness was getting colder in the air, as the blood
was covering the floorboards,
air got colder, as ghosts brushed past me
footsteps followed me, I got so scared I screamed
chills ran down my spine, I got so scared I just at there in silence.

Marie Ward (12)
The Thomas Aveling School

The Deserted House

The house was as creepy as a river of blood
As I walked through the mouldy door
I could hear the groans of zombies like they had just been resurrected
from the dead
As I walked through the narrow corridor the puddles of blood splashed
up my face as I stepped closer to the door
The whistling wind made the curtains blow like wildebeest
on a rampage
I had had enough, I was getting out of there and not coming back.

Lee Routledge (13)
The Thomas Aveling School

The Beach

The blue clouds move smoothly
The sea shines green as it touches the seashore
The golden sand shimmers in the sun
Little islands dotted in view
There is sea surrounding us for miles.

Olivia Lusted (13)
The Thomas Aveling School

The Deserted House

I entered the dark, dark hallway
I felt something cold brush past me
My neck hairs stood up on end

I
Stood
I
Watched
I
Waited
And then
I heard footsteps on the rotting stairs
It was like death tapping on a tombstone

Then . . .

A door opened
Out flew a flock of mystical crows, the smell was atrocious
Then darkness!
A pair of terrifying eyes sat before me
I saw shadows leap from wall to wall
My *hot* body filled with chills . . . I was frightened
I could feel cold, wet blood dripping on my neck like a dripping tap
A smell of dampness filled the air
I could hardly breath
Then those earth shattering voices came
I screamed
I turned
I ran, I was like the wind
It was over, or so I thought . . .

Naomi Moreton-Freeman (12)
The Thomas Aveling School

The Creepy House

The rotten house looks like the Mary Rose
I walk in and I can see damp walls
That are bland and make you feel cold
The rotten furniture is falling apart
They must be centuries old
The creaking floorboards are the same as walking the plank
The bloody axe is laying on the floor
Its reminding me of Henry VIII
The stone-cold dead body stares at me
Like a china doll
The mouldy food is so out of date
It must be centuries old
A jet-black cat is sitting so still, it must be a statue
But its eyes are following me.

Joanne Cooke (12)
The Thomas Aveling School

My Scary Night

Very big screams like a steam train
Pounding footsteps upstairs like dropping bombs
Dead corpse soaking in its own blood
And things eating the person's guts
Windows showing a graveyard as each lightning bolt strikes
Damp puddles making a dripping noise from the roof
A rotting smell of flesh as I enter the basement
Flesh hanging from the walls
Burnt wood smell mixes with the rotting flesh smell
I see a body get up, it's a zombie
'Argh!'
I jump up, I see my room, my bedroom
I get comfortable and fall back to sleep.

Anthony O'Brien (12)
The Thomas Aveling School

Luscious Landscape

Silky sea smashing like a fist breaking a mirror,
Clean sky blowing gently and purely,
Scorching sand scalding the layers of skin of our feet.
Gleaming green far out into the distance.

Peculiar patterns spreading beneath the sand,
Soft clouds like clean, pure wool.
Sizzling sun crisping our warm bodies,
Hefty air meeting our faces with a cool breath.

But there I lay like I was loving every second
Of the surroundings around me.
My toes were pressuring the front of my shoe to let them out
Into the air and so I did.
I laid back and fell into the most comfiest sleeps of my life.

This is what this luscious landscape is like, it is completely
Out of this world!

Matt Tierney (13)
The Thomas Aveling School

Sunny Beach

Bright blue, cloudless sky shining on the sparkly sea
The bright, blazing sun shining down on the calm and relaxed people.

The soft, silky sand spread across the beach
Seaweed lying on the seashore.

Hilltops covered in yellow-golden sand
Deep blue sea slapping against the shore.

The chalk cliffs high above the people
Rocks that surround the cliffs.

Emma Delderfield (13)
The Thomas Aveling School

The Only House

The dust rose from the ground like vampires struggling to get out
from their graves
Floorboards were missing from up the stairs as if people had fallen
through them - into darkness.
Doors were hanging off their hinges as if they were trying to escape
from the spider cobwebs that strangled them
There was no colour in the house
Empty
Cold
Dark
Mysterious
That's all it was
The walls were stone cold, like gravestones being swamped
all over by ivy.
That's what people say the house is like
But nobody is certain.

Jeevan Dhesy (12)
The Thomas Aveling School

The Shore

Walking across the beach,
The sound of the waves crashing against the shore,
Shingle crunching beneath our feet,
Rocks that have fallen scattered across the floor,
Dusk from the late night sky
Can be seen from behind the clouds,
Children playing, their voices can be heard,
People bathing in the cool blue sea,
Beach as far as the eye can see.

Vicki Galle (13)
The Thomas Aveling School

Beach

The exquisite paint work on the yacht reflects perfectly into the glassy
water laps gently up onto the shore,
dragging the golden sands
back down into the sea's depth as it leaves
The great waves bump into the gigantic rocks sending droplets
of salty sea water up as high as the clouds
Silver fish glint in the moonlight as they move quickly into the shadows,
Whenever a gull glides gracefully over the crystal clear water
Crooked old fishing boats bounce up and down on the waves,
Their broken bottoms home to lively crabs and barnacles.
A dog splashes around in the shadows occasionally ducking
under the water to take a better look at the interesting stone.
Finally, the relaxing moonlight gives into the clear
and refreshing sunlight.
Good morning!

Jessica Moreton (14)
The Thomas Aveling School

Broadstairs

Tide-stranded boats sitting on the oil-drenched sand,
The smooth, shiny sea sending its waves crashing upon the shore.
The crab-infested rock pool being revealed as the water level
goes down.
The tall, white cliffs that keep you cool in the shadows as the sun sets.
The scorching sand, bright yellow in the summer sun.
The dreamy smelling café, baking fresh doughnuts and vending cool,
cool ice cream.
The wooden pier at night is home to hundreds of bright,
glistening lights.
Screeching seagulls flying overhead looking for food
dropped by tourists,
And surfers cruising on the tall, curling waves in the Broadstairs Sea.

Andrew King (13)
The Thomas Aveling School

Holiday Beach

Giant trees were towering high,
Soaring birds as high as the clouds.
The cars were as slow as turtles,
The beach glistened in the bright sun.
Sky covered in white, fluffy clouds.
The sound of chattering people,
The rough sea slapping the shore.

Robert Gosling (13)
The Thomas Aveling School

Joss Boy

Curved caves buried beneath
The dusky, murky, lonely mountains.
Seaweed squishing between slimy stones,
Also between my bare toes.
Houses viewing the merciful waves.
The swimmers drifting out to sea.
Jet-skis striking against the unevenness of the waves.

Yvette Marrs (13)
The Thomas Aveling School

The Sea

Dark blue sea crashing onto the shore,
Beaten sand bouncing on the beach.
Battered driftwood lying lifeless on the sand,
Sapphire sky changing as the sun moves up above.
Thin clouds cutting up the blue sky,
White swell like a ghost on top of the turquoise sea.

Oliver Henderson (14)
The Thomas Aveling School

Tell Me Love Is True

At first you were one of them
Walking down the street
Your drum beats on your legs
I never knew one day they would sound so sweet

Love, oh what is love?
Did I feel it for you?
Love, oh what is love?
Tell me love is true

The next time I saw you
You sat in the big chair
Your eyes so bright and shining
With your soft and curly hair

Love, oh what is love?
Did I feel it for you?
Love, oh what is love?
Tell me love is true

The next time we were together
There was a tingling inside
Everything looks so rosy
I was filled with love and pride

Love, oh what is love?
Did I feel it for you?
Love, oh what is love?
Tell me love is true

Four months was how long it lasted
The smiles and the tears
Four months was the brief time we shared
I wish it could have been for years

Love, oh what is love?
Did I feel it for you?
Love, oh what is love?
Tell me love is true

All those happy times
Were not so long ago
Soft words you sung still strong
You were my hero, did you know?

Love, oh what is love?
Did I feel it for you?
Love, oh what is love?
Tell me love is true

I now see you walking down the street
I see you on the bus
I see you with all the other girls
Tell me . . . what happened to us?

Jodie Phelps (15)
The Thomas Aveling School

Little Sister

Your tiny fingers, tiny toes,
big blue eyes and little button nose.
Your tiny body in your cot,
the little noise you made when you'd cried a lot.
The first time you giggled,
the first time you laughed,
the first time you hugged that little giraffe.
All these things I remember about you,
because little sister, I love you through and through.

You're one in a million and I think you're quite cool,
considering you've only just started playschool.
And now that you're three, going on four, I think you're
smarter than ever before.
You give me cuddles and kisses too,
we even both like Winnie The Pooh.
You jump up and down when I walk in the door,
and I don't even mind when you're asleep and you snore.
So here little sister, this poem's for you,
so I can show how much I love and care about you.

Emma Williams (15)
The Thomas Aveling School

I'm Not Alone

I'm in my deserted house
I'm not alone
I can hear footsteps as I walked along the creaking floorboards
I could hear screaming
The noise came louder as the ghosts came closer
It was like a roaring lion
I'm not alone!
The cobwebs made me shiver as they tickled my face
I was shivering with fear
The dampness is invading my house
I'm not alone!
Blood is dripped down the walls
It's as red as a rose
The light came on
I'm not alone!

Jade Minchin (12)
The Thomas Aveling School

Untitled

Tear me from your heart, tearing me apart.
Marie is my love in vain, when my blood bleeds sweeter,
Thank the night air's rain.

When you pray, searching for good
Do you cry yourself to sleep?
When you laugh, self-made joke,
Is the joy so hard to keep?
Angel in flight, demon in night,
Tearing me apart, you stole my heart.
When we kiss, sharing joy,
Is it hard to know I'm in eternal sleep?

Adam Leighton (15)
The Thomas Aveling School

The Terrifying House

The creaking of the doors were as loud as a firework,
Footsteps following me.
Everywhere I went,
I felt wind like mice rushing round my feet.

I heard whispering of children running around,
Chills ran down my spine as the shadows walked round me.
There was screaming in the wind,
As I walked round the terrifying house.

Cobwebs covered my face,
As I walked up the stairs.
Eyes were on the walls,
Everywhere I went.

The darkness turned to light,
As ghosts filled up the room.
I turned cold,
As the ghosts brushed past me.

Amy Witcher (12)
The Thomas Aveling School

The Rippled Sand

The rippled sand at my feet
As I watch the clear sky and water meet

When the high hills are in the background
Layers of clouds hover over the horizon

Distant views of people the size of peas
Standing above the glimmering seas.

Sam Martin (13)
The Thomas Aveling School

Your Worst Nightmare House

I got pushed through the old, damp door
The wind pushed me through
Everything was as damp as a wet cloth,
The creaking of the door was like someone screaming for help
I could hear footsteps going step by step, like a huge tiger
There was no escape from here
I could see ghosts gleaming at me
They looked like a tall, white sheet
The blood on the floor was as red as a rose
The bodies looked like dead fish
Everything was as dirty as mould
I stepped one step forward
The smell got worse like gone-off fish and cabbage
I got chills up and down my spine
I didn't know what to do
I didn't know how to get out of there.

Manika Nagar (13)
The Thomas Aveling School

Market Place, Bodrum, Turkey

The massive market place is packed solid and blaring
The clothes blowing about in the sea breeze
The multicolour of canopies hanging high overhead
All different people selling and bartering for products
Starving dogs chase skinny cats around the harbour
Small cats get underfoot, hiding in the stalls.

The different smells of foreign food intoxicate the senses
Shopkeepers pester you, like a fly that won't go away
When you step out, the noise dies away like a firework
A dog runs past after a cat, as you walk back to the hotel.

Luke Murphy (14)
The Thomas Aveling School

Portugal

Portugal is where I went on holiday this year,
People walking around the market place.
The happy look upon their face.
The yachts out of the docks still in first gear.

I can hear the fountain - drip, drop.
Parties starting late at night,
Drinks served to their delight,
But when the parties come to a stop
Portugal is silent.

People sleeping, people dreaming.
Portugal sleeping, still,
Until the next morning.

Robbie Harris (13)
The Thomas Aveling School

Number 56

The dust was like a white coat covering the house,
Shadows grew through the house like an old oak tree,
The cold made a shiver run down my spine,
As mist swarmed through the house like the black death,
And blood covered the floor like a rapid, red river of wine.
Suddenly, the squeaking floorboards squeaked a viscous noise,
Then *bang!*
   Bang!
      Bang!
I turned, he's down the stairs,
I screamed, he's gone!

Susan Hawkes (12)
The Thomas Aveling School

Autumn Days

A utumn trees are really bare
U nder trees is full of leaves
T rees are blowing in the wind
U sually it is very windy
M ostly people stay at home
N ear their nice, warm fires

D ays get colder and colder
A t about October
Y ou can feel the wind on your face
S tay at home in October.

Alan Rowe (11)
The Thomas Aveling School

Autumn Poem

Golden sun in the aqua sky.
People surfing on the sea.
The wind pushing to and fro.
Leaves blowing on the path.

Steven Lowrey (11)
The Thomas Aveling School

Diving

Fish as colourful as rainbows,
The water was crystal clear.
Rocks clothed in seaweed,
Bubbles dribbling to the surface,
The current swift but calm.
The sand clean as can be.

Joe Garofalo (13)
The Thomas Aveling School

Deserted House

I can hear the wind howl
The screams are terrifying
I can see black shadows
I'm not alone.

The smells are weird like rotten flesh
There are pools of blood beneath my feet
Someone's watching me
I can hear footsteps creeping towards me.

It's freaking me out
I opened the damp, wooden door
It slammed shut behind me
As I sprint out of the deserted house.

Rebecca Minchin (12)
The Thomas Aveling School

The Horrifying House

The cobwebs shook like bags of marbles.
There were bodies like the insides of frogs.
Mice scampered across the floor like shooting stars above my head.
Rats piled up as tall as mountains.
Thick pieces of food and crumbs lay on the floor.
The spiders moved like light-footed elephants.
Their eyes sagged like bags of blood.
The doors sounded like shattering rulers.
In the garden there were apples the size of Frankentein's head
and the grass was as tall as six foot legs.
All of a sudden the house shook like a rattlesnake's tail.
I ran.

Sean Holbrook (12)
The Thomas Aveling School

Old Haunted House

The old haunted house was cold as I entered
Shadows were all around
It's as dark as the winter nights
Blood as the company for the shadows
As the floorboards creak and groan talking to the shadows
They replied by moving and banging
The wind whistled through the open doors
It smelt empty
A thick layer of dust like a sheet of snow lay on the dusty fireplace.

Nicola Dadswell (12)
The Thomas Aveling School

Autumn Colours

Autumn leaves so beautiful
in their final stage.
Now all the creatures in the world
are going to sleep.
Golden colours cover the land
as autumn creeps in.
People huddle round the fire
in the hope that they will not feel the chill.

Oliver Homewood (11)
The Thomas Aveling School

My Beach

Cliffs white, like a blank canvas,
The sun magnificent, glowing with crimson rays.
Surf high, crashing onto the sapphire sea,
The sky cloudless and blue, like ink on a forgotten page.
Sand golden, falling through my hands, like old lost treasures.

Holly Crundwell (14)
The Thomas Aveling School

The House

The creaking of the boards
The slamming of the doors
The mist is rising
It is wondering
The doors creak, the doors slam, they are closed
The screams reach peak
The cold rises, the mist is forming
It is decaying
All the windows are jammed
All the doors are slammed
The cockroaches are coming through the door
A splash of blood, it strikes
I fall, the hard floor is cold
He has taken me.

Max Burford (13)
The Thomas Aveling School

Number 56

A set of cracks covered the wall,
Filled with a rot of many colours,
Moistness of mould filled the air, and
Left me to darkness and to scare,
The room of litter was a bin,
Covered in blood from flesh or man,
The moist, wet wood broke slowly
The reclining door moved slickly
And scraggly chairs clicked loudly
Old torn books of no value scattered on the floor
Below the windows where no light is received.

Tom Patching (12)
The Thomas Aveling School

Who Said Love Was Only A Feeling?

Who said love was only a feeling?
Love is the fuel that drives my heart,
It's the drug my body craves,
But yet you say, 'Can we just be friends?'

I've been summoning the courage for weeks
To ask you to be my love,
All I hear are these ill-fated words,
'Can we just be friends?'

I love you,
Why can't you love me?
These words divide us like that wall that divided
Thisbie and her fair Pyramus,
Can we just be *bloody* friends?

But can we just be friends?
I mean, my love for you is so strong,
You are my world,
You are my sole reason for life,
We can't just be friends.

I love you Megan, I love you,
Only you can make me complete,
That's why I wrote this for *you,* you my darling
Make me the happiest man alive,
Be mine.

David Pullen (15)
The Thomas Aveling School

I Am The Cheetah

I am a cheetah.
Skilful, sophisticated and swift.
I am agile; I can turn corners in clouds of dust.
I am better than any sports car.
Nought to sixty in seconds, that's me.
You think I am beautiful, sleek and magical.
The males think I am a beautiful killer.
I tower over them with my skill.
I'm a sprinter, I could out-run Paula Radcliffe if I tried.
I would probably end up eating her first though.
I like hunting.
Fending for myself.
Antelope and gazelle are my favourite.
My pack and I killed an elephant.
It went well . . . for a while.
We were skilful; we pounced, rounded, ripped and tugged.
It put up a fight.
A dust cloud of jaws and claws.
It stamped. It was vicious. We got it, but someone died.
Our leader, Swipe, my one true love.
He was happy, content and very handsome.
He rose above me.
Now I'm the leader.
I'm a bit of a show-off.
Why not?
I like to live life to the limit.

Jasmine Conkie (13)
The Thomas Aveling School

The Butterfly, Me And The Bee

The butterfly I saw, was lying on the floor,
When it saw me, it wanted to flee
For it had seen a *great . . . big . . .*
Bee!

Elizabeth Dalgleish (11)
Townley Grammar School For Girls

A Testing Time

My lucky mascot's down on the floor.
And I'm getting nervous more and more.
The desk's split up. We're getting ready.
My heart rate's fast. Gotta keep it steady.
As the teacher drones on about the test.
I concentrate hard on doing my best.
And now the test's started. I'm at the right pace.
I hear calls of the time. Against time it's a race.
Questions and answers and multiple choice.
And inside my head beats the bellowing voice:
You've got to keep going it's nearly all done
Fifteen minutes and then you've won.
The questions were hard some needed more thinking.
The page is a blur my eyes keep on blinking.
Seven more questions then it's all back to normal.
Schools easy once more. No more tests. It's all *formal!*
I've completed the answers.
It's over at last!
I check it all over but got to check fast.
I watch as the second hand hits the 12 digits.
We're told the test's finished and everyone fidgets.

Some time later we're handed a letter.
Have I done well or maybe better.
As I went home my results, I saw.
I'd passed by 45, 46 plus more.
I was over the moon about my success.
I've got good marks and sat the tests.
I smile to myself but won't make a fuss.
I've only passed my eleven plus!

Katie Caserta (11)
Townley Grammar School For Girls

Older Sister

No, I can't do your homework
I cannot divide,
No, I can't solve your problems
You're older than I!

No, I hated your boyfriend
He wasn't a nice bloke,
No, the people at work
Don't think you're a joke!

No, you're not getting fat
And you don't look a state,
No, of course you're not ugly
In fact, you look great!

Now come on sister
Leave me alone,
I'm so glad next week
She's leaving home!

Lauren Hill (13)
Townley Grammar School For Girls

My Friend And His Crave!

I had a friend called Dave,
He often had a crave,
His crave was not normal,
Nor was it very formal.
But I have to say,
It made him so gay.
He went to jump and shout,
But he said nowt.
And this was the end of Dave
And his silly old crave!

Emily Thoroughgood (12)
Townley Grammar School For Girls

A Snail's Tail

Hello, I'm a snail,
I feel I should tell this tale,
Told from a house's wall,
About a warrior, proud and tall.

There was once a man,
He sold ham,
He never yelled, 'Yuck, loads of snails,'
He never stepped on kitty-cat's tails.

He cared for every living thing,
I feel it my duty his tale to sing,
About his final stand,
About his gentle, loving hand.

A war was on, he was called to fight,
He had to leave in the middle of the night,
His daughter and son started to cry,
They did not understand why.

He stroked his daughter's hair
And swung her round, in the air,
He gently tickled her chin
And for bed that night, tucked her in.

His son he held very tight,
Their tears mingled in the night,
He said, 'Be brave,'
His son replied, 'You sound so grave.'

He hugged his wife,
Said he would write every day of his life,
While he was away,
She promised single she would stay.

He left his family with the words,
'I am off to help the soldier herds,
There is a problem with Iraq
And I fear I shall not ever come back.'

He left in tears on the next plane,
His family's tears fell like rain,
The little girl cried, 'I want Daddy,'
Her mum replied, 'I know you do Maddy.'

There is a sad end to this tale,
Brought to you by a snail,
There was a problem with Iraq
And this soldier never came back.

Jenny Hunt
Townley Grammar School For Girls

Alone

I'm all by myself
I'm all alone.
There's nobody here,
I'm all on my own.

Why does no one care?
No one should be alone
Does no body know?
That I'm on my own.

I'm thinking of them.
But they're not thinking of me
Nobody cares.
That I want to be free.

I need a friend,
But there's no one here
I need someone
To take away my fear.

I'm all by myself
I'm all alone.
There's nobody here,
I'm all on my own.

Laura Pauli (12)
Townley Grammar School For Girls

Why?

Why is my little sister so annoying?
And why does she moan and groan?
Why is life so boring?
Most things never known.

Why is the sky so blue?
But black in the middle of the night?
Why do we feel so down
And suddenly become so bright?

Why is food and drink so important
To our lives every day?
Why does the boat come into the harbour
And why does a car park in the bay?

I know I sound like a baby
Asking things still to learn.
But these things inside my head
Are beginning to turn.

Jordan Louise Emery (11)
Townley Grammar School For Girls

I Haven't Done My Homework Because . . .

I saw a zombie heading for the stair,
Then I started floating high up in the air.
I pulled myself together and fell flat on the floor,
Then, what's that I see? A lion's incisor jaw!

I picked up the jaw and took it to my room,
Where there, I found a walking, talking broom!
'Look over there!' the broom excitedly said,
'I think that's your homework on the bed!'

As I went to pick it up, the zombie reappeared,
I jumped with trepidation and my homework disappeared!

Christine Roberts (11)
Townley Grammar School For Girls

She

If she were furniture, she would be a bed,
because she is comforting and soft, once you get used to her.

If she were a flower, she would be a rose,
because she can be harmful, yet so delicate.

If she were a colour, she would be multicoloured,
because she is different every minute.

If she were a film, she would be Romeo and Juliet,
because the film is full of love, just like her heart.

If she were music, she would be 'You To Me Are Everything',
because this is what she feels to someone close.

If she were a meal, she would be fruit,
because it can be colourful just like her personality.

If she were weather, she would be lightning,
because you never know when she would strike with her love.

If she were a scent, she would be lavender,
because it's fresh and keeps everyone smiling.

If she were a word, she would be love,
as this is what she expresses to everyone.

If she were time, she would be evening,
because it's peaceful and lazy just like her.

If she were an animal, she would be a bird,
because then she could fly around and check everyone is happy.

If she were a country, she would be Italy,
because this is the country of love.

If she were a house, she would be the one in the centre of the world,
so then everyone knows she is there.

If she were a book, she would be Princess Diaries,
because a princess is what she is to me.

If she were a name, she would be Mum.

Ramiren Vedash (12)
Townley Grammar School For Girls

Patsy Pelzer - Paying A Painful Price

(This poem is based on a character from 'A Child Called It' trilogy by Dave Pelzer)

Empty.
Deprived.
Like the sapphire, salty tear that is the ocean.
Deprived of love. Deprived of care. Deprived of feeling.
But only on the surface
And to the clean-cut idiocy of my human eyes.
For if I had seen with my now cruelly shattered heart from the
beginning,
I would not now be lying here with my eyes open to the heavens,
Staring at the cold, flat ceiling,
While lying on my stone plateau of a bed.

As a tear drops to my cheek,
I think of what brought me to my loss.
Hatred, jealousy.
But most of all; fear, no not fear,
Utmost terror.

The bitter, salty tear touches my lips, as I freeze with sadness.
Thoughts and memories pass through my mind as if played by an
imaginary projector
And tears silently begin to spill down my face while the pain of that
past lifetime rush back to me.
Like a horse galloping roughly but gracefully through a field full of
buttercups and barley.

His fear, his hatred for his mother had pushed him to work so hard,
For so little appreciation.
But it was his narrow-mindedness that had forced him to believe that
things would get better.

I feel the pain.
I feel the sheer stabbing into my heart as he tells me he will leave
again and again.

Even if I attempt to help.

Now I am the one filled with hatred.

I strain to stop crying as my body tenses.
I will show him that I can make it.
That without him I am still strong.
After all, through all those past years I stayed alive . . .

Bianca Lee (15)
Townley Grammar School For Girls

The Lioness

She leaps, she pounces, she runs, she hunts,
A lioness on the prowl.
The proud mother of three young cubs,
She flaunts a murderous scowl.

Lying in the undergrowth, she spots her prey
And plans her killing route.
An elegant mistress of the trade,
Which she does so well suit.

The chase ensues, post-haste she springs,
Maintains a winning glare.
And closing in, inspects her feed,
Enough for all to share.

A leap, so swift, with grace and style,
She collars her tasty meal.
Then comes padding from their hide,
The kids, to claim their deal

Lucy Haslam (15)
Townley Grammar School For Girls

Water

Trickling slyly from the sky,
The water, comes creeping, like from an eye,
As time passes it becomes quite steady,
But gets more impatient and becomes heavy.

Children run in with their clothes drenched,
Looking like they ran into a puddled trench,
They took outside to the gloomy clouds,
As they grumble out loud.

The water drops are as clear as crystal,
Gliding downwards they gleam,
Some drop into rivers
And some into streams.

Drip, drip I sense its presence,
Such a thing of pure beauty,
Clear and cool as crystal.

Devina Patel (11)
Townley Grammar School For Girls

Why?

Why wars? Why fights? Why hunger and pain?
Why droughts in poor countries? Why don't they get rain?
Why can't there be more happiness and sharing?
Why can't our world be much more caring?
Why can't everyone just get along?
Why does everyone keep doing wrong?
Why do people cause such harm?
Can't they sit still, think, try to be calm?
Does anyone else feel like I do?
And wish, wish the world wasn't quite so blue?
I dream of a world, where there is no bad,
All will be peaceful, content and glad.

Millie Ratcliff (12)
Townley Grammar School For Girls

The Way I See It

Please help us God above,
To change this world enough,
So I don't have to ask,
Where is the love?

What happened to humanity?
Why is there poverty?
Why are people dying?
You should listen to me.

People killed 'cause they're black,
Talking behind their back,
What is it with racism?
Everyday there's an attack.

What happened to equality?
Can't we leave these people be?
Leave this world in peace,
Just listen here to me.

People out there sick and starving,
Children in their hundreds dying,
This world should be united
And stop this stupid fighting.

We shouldn't be at war,
The dying and the poor,
Are calling to us in their numbers,
They need our help for sure.

Please help us God above,
To change this world enough,
So I don't have to ask,
Where is the love?

This world should be united
And stop this stupid fighting.
Where is the love?

Faith Youngman (13)
Townley Grammar School For Girls

Why Mum, Why?

Mum . . .
Why do birds fly in the sky, Mum?
Why not in the sea?
Can only birds fly, Mum?
Or can you and me?
Why do we have five fingers, Mum?
Why not two or four?
Can you only count to a hundred, Mum?
I can count to more!
Why are you holding your head, Mum?
Why are you taking that pill?
Now, you're lying down, Mum,
Mum, are you ill?
Mum?
Mum?
Why Mum, why?

Laura Daniels (12)
Townley Grammar School For Girls

Greedy Mr Strood

Greedy Mr Strood likes his food, this is what he does;
He cries for pies,
He begs for eggs,
He fakes for cakes,
He licks his poodle for a noodle,
He works hard for lard,
He competes for sweets,
He wails for quails,
He wheezes for cheeses,
He keeps on lickin' just for chicken,
He gets all shaken for a rasher of bacon,
He pays a fee for a single pea,
He's rather unpleasant for a pheasant,
He wears a wig to eat a pig,
But when he's quiet, he's on a diet.

Serena Raphael (11)
Townley Grammar School For Girls

A Mad Scientist's Briefcase

In a mad scientist's briefcase, you may find,
Springs of all different shapes and kinds.

Toenail clippings from his feet that smell
And an Elvis wig - with loads of gel.

A false teeth nicker, to nick false teeth
And a hand which belonged to an ape called Keith.

Some elastic bands to flick at other people,
Plus a ning-nong as high as a steeple.

A peachypeachypoo that actually flies
And some different coloured googley eyes.

A funky hat to make you look weird
And a picture of his sister, who grew a beard.

And now it's time for me to go,
Did you like my poem? Please say no!

Loretta Gay (11)
Townley Grammar School For Girls

The Cheetah's Pounce

The cheetah, a sly and spotty creature,
Searches for its prey.
He smells it, he follows its scent,
He moves, as quick as greased lightning,
As he runs, the green of the jungle is just a blur.

He picks out the doe and corners her, ready to pounce,
He pounces, a flash of yellow and brown,
The large creature that he is, bites into his victim,
Her innocent blood is spilt,
It oozes out of her wound, as warm and crimson as ever,
He growls one more time before finishing her off.

The cheetah, sly as a fox,
Quick as greased lightning.

Ann-Julie Gibbs (12)
Townley Grammar School For Girls

What Should I Write?

Poems are a wonder,
Oh! an ode to joy,
A page filled with magic,
For every girl and boy.

Oh, how I love to write,
My feelings all engage,
But there's a tiny problem,
Of how to fill the page.

Should it be filled with anger,
Or should it be warm and gentle?
Should the page be filled with cheer,
Or should I just go mental?

Should it be a limerick,
Or maybe a haiku?
Should my poem be free verse,
Or couplets, rhyming twos?

Should it have a rhythm?
Should it have a rhyme?
Should it be an analogue,
Or should it be in time?

Should the pace be very fast,
Or extremely slow?
Should the tone of voice for this poem,
Vary from high to low?

Should I use alliteration,
Or should it be a shape?
Should I use some metaphors,
Or just sit there and gape?

Oh, I don't know what to do,
I'm yet to be inspired!
But I think that you must admit,
This poem will be admired!

So next time you're stuck on writing a page,
Read my suggestions and prevent a rage!

Carla Smith (13)
Townley Grammar School For Girls

All The Goodness Of A Garden

Step in the garden and smell the air,
Sweet as a rose though I must be fair,
There are some weeds but only a few,
Out in the garden there's plenty to do.
Dandelions they're bobbing their heads,
As they sway back and forth and have I said,
The best are bleeding hearts, red and white,
A good combination, that looks great at night.
Tell me now and tell me the truth,
Did you see anything better in all your youth?
When you're feeling bad or just plain blue,
Your garden's the best thing to comfort you.
Now how can I forget the water feature,
Whether it's a statue of a human or a creature,
It gives that touch all gardens need,
Spend time in your garden and do a good deed.
There's nothing more that I can say,
But spend time in your garden every day!

Zara Mohsin (12)
Townley Grammar School For Girls

Autumn

Autumn is arriving, the leaves are turning brown,
Crumpling and sliding, falling all around.
The nights are getting colder, the frost sets on the car,
Put your woolly coats on, the winter's not that far.
The trees are turning bare, the ducks are flying south,
When you go outside, frost comes out your mouth.
The sun is going down, setting in the sky,
Yellow, gold and orange, watching the world go by.

Lizzy Varley (11)
Townley Grammar School For Girls